OTHER PAPERBACK TITLES OF INTEREST

The Elements of Grammar
Margaret D. Shertzer

The Elements of Editing
Arthur Plotnik

The Elements of Correspondence
Mary A. De Vries

The Elements of Speechwriting and Public Speaking
Jeff Scott Cook

The Elements of Business Writing
Gary Blake and Robert W. Bly

The Elements of Legal Writing
Martha Faulk and Irving M. Mehler

The Elements of Nonsexist Usage
Val Dumond

The Elements of Technical Writing
Gary Blake and Robert W. Bly

The Elements of Playwriting
Louis. E. Catron

The Art of Questioning
Peter Megargee Brown

*How to Write a Children's Book and
Get It Published*
Barbara Seuling

The Elements of Screenwriting

Books by Irwin R. Blacker

NOVELS

Westering
Days of Gold
Taos
The Kilroy Gambit
Search and Destroy
Chain of Command
To Hell in a Basket
The Middle of the Fire
Standing on a Drum

ANTHOLOGIES

Irregulars, Partisans, Guerrillas
The Old West in Fiction
The Old West in Fact
Prescott's Histories: The Rise and Decline
   of the Spanish Empire
Hakluyt's Voyages
The Book of Books: A Treasury of Great Bible Fiction
Conquest: Dispatches of Cortez from the New World
   (with Harry Rosen)
The Golden Conquistadores (with Harry Rosen)
Directors at Work (with Bernard Kantor and Anne Kramer)

CHILDREN'S BOOKS

The Bold Conquistadores
Cortes and the Aztec Conquest

THE
ELEMENTS
OF
SCREENWRITING

━━━

A Guide for Film and Television Writers

Irwin R. Blacker

MACMILLAN • USA

Macmillan General Reference
A Simon & Schuster Macmillan Company
1633 Broadway
New York, NY 10019-6785

Library of Congress Cataloging-in-Publication Data
Blacker, Irwin R.
    The elements of screenwriting / Irwin R. Blacker.
        p.   cm.
    Includes index.
    ISBN 0-02-861450-X (pbk.)
    1. Motion picture authorship.   2. Television authorship.
    I. Title.
    PN1996.B5   1996
    808.2'3—dc20   96-18961
                                                        CIP

10   9   8   7   6   5   4   3   2   1

Printed in the United States of America

ACKNOWLEDGMENTS

My debts are large: to Aristotle, first, foremost, and always; then to Elder Olson, Eric Bentley, and Bernard Grebanier; and to the sixty-eight classes and one hundred and thirty-six sessions at the University of Southern California in which I discussed these principles with students—graduate and undergraduate—who in turn taught me much.

My debt to thousands of films and film scripts is also large. Good films and scripts teach us much, as do those whose visible seams and flaws reveal more than many appreciate.

CONTENTS

PREFATORY NOTE

Irwin Blacker did not believe that creativity could be taught. He did, however, believe that the fundamentals of the craft of screenwriting—structure, plot, dialogue, exposition, and character—could be.

Professor Blacker gathered these principles from many sources and distilled them over many years. Irwin Blacker had over forty years of experience as a radio dramatist, screenwriter, television documentary and dramatic writer, television story editor, and novelist. He had a keen scholarly interest in epic poetry, contemporary American and Elizabethan drama, the Arthurian tales, and—above all—the classic Greek theater. His students, therefore, received from him the hard discipline of the modern American film and also that deep and abiding sense of structure that underlies all dramatic narrative.

Honed to their most concise form, the elements are largely taken from his introductory course at the University of Southern California. In that class students were required to attend the lectures and then to construct a narrative in synopsis and treatment form. In the advanced class each student presented an arrangement of scenes for his or her proposed script. For two hours after the presentation he or she was not permitted to speak while, one by one, the remainder of the class answered the questions: Would you buy this film if you were a producer? Why? Why not?

It was not a class for the timid, the academic, or the person interested in self-indulgent expression or "transcending the genre." And it could be a painful experience even if, like myself, one had the otherwise pleasurable honor of being the professor's son-in-law. But it was a necessary passage through fire, because Professor Blacker knew full well that the day his students left his class they would have to function as professionals in a difficult and risky business.

Irwin Blacker's death prevented him from completing *The Elements of Screenwriting*. His wife, Ethel H. Blacker, his daughter, Deborah E. B. Weiner, and I have, therefore, taken some of the material from his notes for the manuscript and checked it against tape recordings of his class lectures and the notebooks of his teaching assistant, Peter Rothenberg. In arranging the material, we have followed Professor Blacker's outline. We have not added or changed the text; where differences existed between his notes, the tapes, and the class notes, we chose the most apt rendering of the point under discussion. The format, however, is Professor Blacker's and the writing is his.

Professor Blacker's extraordinary success as a teacher was a result of his demand for a high standard of performance, his insight into the capabilities of individual students, and his teaching method, condensed into the principles of this textbook. It may not be too much to suggest that his students' success as film directors, screenwriters, story editors, and film teachers has been his ultimate tribute.

—Steven H. Weiner, 1986

PREFACE

The purpose of this book is to explain what a film script is and how one is written. No author or teacher can teach someone else how to be creative or how to find inspiration. However, technique and a professional approach to the creative form can be taught. The difference between a carpenter and a cabinetmaker is a matter of technique. Likewise, the way a screenplay is put together is technique and can be learned. The teacher can't give students an ear for dialogue, but he can show the differences between good and bad dialogue. He can't teach students how to invent a plot, but he can teach them to see the flaws and weaknesses of a plot. He can teach techniques of exposition, how to build a scene, a crisis, and a climax, and how to identify the conflict and develop character.

The scriptwriter can learn the basic principles of dramaturgy. There are no absolute rules or laws for the dramaturgy of the screenplay; however, there are 2,500 years of dramatic analysis and tens of thousands of dramatic films from which principles can be derived. Styles and conventions in drama have changed from the Greeks to the Elizabethans to the Victorians to the Modernists as influenced by Freud, but although a few interesting and successful screenplays have been designed to find alternative principles, the basic theory of Aristotelian dramaturgy has not been superseded by any basic reforms.

In the arts, the simple fact that an experiment has been made seems to impress and satisfy many critics; it should not. At the very least, the writer should know the collective wisdom concerning screen dramaturgy before he tries to defy it. Experimentation is needed and new forms and techniques are something every artist strives for, but there must be some discipline. In art as in science, experimentation must have a purpose, and the mere statement, "this is an experimental script," does not make it *ipso facto* a success. The writer who seeks alternatives by experimenting would do well to know the traditions first so that he is experimenting on something and not on nothing. Difference from basic principles alone is not enough; the experimenter should define what the experiment is attempting to accomplish. Dr. Edward C. Kendall, the Nobel laureate who discovered cortisone, said that he found 4,300 ways in which cortisone could *not* be made before he discovered the way in which it could.

I lean heavily on Aristotle's *Poetics*, the best single analysis of what a play is. The *Poetics* seems an unusual place to begin a book on the film script, but there are many reasons for anyone writing films to know and understand this small essay. Over two thusand years old and written with a limited number of plays as the source of its analysis, the *Poetics* remains the first and probably the best attempt to understand what a play is and why it works. Much of this mere 10,000-word essay does not even relate to drama; none of it, obviously, related to film, but at its core are ideas which must be taken into account by any playwright or scriptwriter today. Many of the words and phrases of Aristotle seem obscure today, and they may even have been obscure to Aristotle's contemporaries, but there remains a core of understanding that has not yet been surpassed. From Aristotle's time to our own, dramatic structure has remained basically the same. All that has followed since on the subject has been commentary.

As there is no common frame of reference, no body of films known to all, I will cite certain classics and popular films in the hope that the reader will be familiar with some or most of them.

A screenplay is simply a blueprint for making a film. The word *playwright* has a particular significance in relation to this when one remembers that *wright* means "one who works, makes, or constructs." A script is made; it is put together with parts. A Shakespearean script averages thirty-five scenes—crises or confrontations—places in the script where a character acts or makes a decision, or makes a decision not to act or not to make a decision. In a 100-minute dramatic film there are twenty-four to twenty-six such scenes. The making of a script involves the selection and ordering of these scenes in the most effective way.

The structure of the script takes into account the following:

Plot—The ordering and selection of scenes to tell a story and affect an audience.

Character—The particulars that bring individuals to life within the context of the plot.

Conflict—The driving factor.

Crisis—The point at which the story can go in one direction or another.

Climax—The most important crisis.

Exposition—What a viewer must know, and when.

Dialogue—Its nature, its values, and its limitations.

These are the elements this book is about.

Anyone writing film, anyone directing, producing, editing, viewing, writing about it, or teaching it should know these basic elements.

There are secondary aspects to scriptwriting, such as the look of a script as a blueprint; the business of film as craft, industry, and art; production considerations, and the forms of the synopsis, treatment, and adaptation. These are all important aspects of scriptwriting, though they are secondary to conflict, plot, structure, character, exposition, and dialogue. This book is organized into two parts, with individual chapters on the primary elements followed by chapters on the secondary aspects.

The storyteller was the outlaw on Parnassus because he was not included in the original cast of Greek muses; the scriptwriter is the outlaw's illegitimate child. That does not mean that because his ancestry is clouded, he is any less than any other artist, but merely that he is different and his problems are different. The screenwriter has an important place in the making of a film. Few producers or directors will say otherwise, though critics might. The proof of the script is not in where the director places his camera or what music backs a scene or what star plays the lead part, but in the story the writer has selected to be told verbally and visually. While a good script does not necessarily make a good film, it is absolutely true that no great film was ever made from a bad script.

—Irwin R. Blacker

Part 1

CHAPTER 1

<h1 style="text-align:center">Definitions</h1>

ANTAGONIST. Adversary or opponent of the protagonist; enemy or villain.

ANTI-HERO. A protagonist who lacks the stature or virtues of the traditional Aristotelian hero.

BEGINNING. The point in the script before which nothing need have taken place; information relevant to the story about earlier action can be presented in *exposition*.

CATHARSIS. According to Aristotle, the purging of pity or terror by viewing a tragedy; in film, the relieving of emotional tensions.

CAUSAL RELATIONSHIP. The *conflict* takes place because something happens or has happened. Each *crisis* in turn takes place because of an earlier action or decision or failure to act or decide. Action and *conflict* or *crisis* have a causal relationship.

CINEMA VERITÉ. A form of documentary film in which a small, hand-held camera is used to record scenes under natural conditions.

CLICHÉ. (From the French word for a stereotype plate, a block for printing.) Hence, any expression, or, in film, any technique or convention that has been used so often it has lost its freshness and its effectiveness.

CLIMAX. The highest point of interest and tension; the *crisis* in which the complications are reversed and the *conflict* resolved.

COMEDY. Drama with a happy ending or non-tragic theme; a humorous treatment of character and situation.

COMPLICATION. Sometimes called "rising action"; those parts

3

of the plot which make the relationships and *conflicts* complex; the tying of the knot that will be untied in the *climax* and *resolution*.

CONFLICT. That which takes place when two or more forces come into opposition physically, mentally, or emotionally.

CRISIS. A point in the *plot* requiring action or decision to resolve or to fail to resolve part of the *conflict*, causing realignment of forces or some change in the *protagonist*.

CROSS-PLOT. Breakdown of shooting script into days, locations, number of pages, or scenes to be shot per day; a tool used in budgeting and scheduling shooting.

DENOUEMENT or RESOLUTION. The falling action of the screenplay, where all problems not resolved in the *climax* are unraveled and any needed explanation takes place.

DEUS EX MACHINA. (From the Latin for "god out of the machine.") An entity who appeared in classical plays to resolve the conflict. In film, any character or event brought in arbitrarily or artificially to solve the problem or a solution reached illogically; e.g., the cavalry arrives unexpectedly in the nick of time.

DIALOGUE. Conversation between two or more people that advances the plot.

DRAMA. (From the Greek *dran*, meaning "to do" or "to act.") In film, a story of human *conflict* told through a series of related events.

EFFECT. The desired response from the viewer that the script is structured to elicit.

END. The point in the script where nothing need follow. The *conflict* has been resolved and all *complications* explained.

ENTERTAINMENT. (From the Latin *tenare*, meaning "to grab" or "to hold.") The least the viewer has the right to demand of a screenplay.

EPIPHANY. The unexpected action that comes as a shock, but which, in retrospect, makes sense in its context.

EXPOSITION. Those parts of the script that present what has happened before and identify the characters, the time and place of the action, and the relationship of the characters.

HUBRIS. Excessive pride, ambition, or overconfidence that brings down the hero of a tragedy; a basic flaw in the hero.

4

INCIDENT. An episode presented as a single, continuous action in which something takes place or a decision is made, usually having its own internal *crisis*.

MASTER SCENE. All the action and *dialogue* that takes place within one setting at one time.

MIDDLE. That part of the script after the *conflict* is locked and before it is resolved, where the *crises* rise to a *climax*.

MIMESIS. Imitation; art imitates life.

MOIRA. (Greek for "destiny" or "fate.") The Greeks did not believe man has free will or choice; the outcome is predetermined by *moira*.

PLAYWRIGHT. From the Old English *wright*, meaning "work"; an artificer who makes or constructs by means of labor or art; thus, "play-maker."

PLOT. A planned series of interrelated actions that take place because of the interplay of one force upon another through the struggle of the opposing forces to a *climax* and *resolution*.

POETICS. In the Aristotelian sense, "making" or "to make."

PROTAGONIST. The main *character* around whom action takes place; the hero.

REVERSAL. A change in the fortunes of the *protagonist*.

STORYBOARD. Sketches of scenes prepared for the director in preproduction planning.

SUBPLOT. A story line secondary to the central *plot;* preferably, one related to it.

SUSPENSE. The uncertainty and anticipation about what is going to happen next and how the events will affect one or more of the *characters*.

THEME. An intellectual abstraction; the idea that unifies the structure and is represented by the actions of the *characters* as a whole dramatic piece.

TRAGEDY. According to Aristotle, a play with a tragic ending brought on by fate or a flaw in the hero. Today we define tragedy as any story with serious problems leading to an unhappy or disastrous ending.

UNITY. An organizing principle that relates the parts to the whole; relates everything to the theme.

CHAPTER 2

Conflict

The premise is the basis of the conflict

The premise must be clear to the writer before he begins to write the script, although it will not be stated in the script. The concept of the premise can usually be described in one sentence. If it takes two or more, it may be about too many things and confused.

> What is the premise of *King Lear?* "Blind trust leads to destruction."
>
> What is the premise of *Macbeth?* "Ambition leads to its own destruction."
>
> What is the premise of a typical Hollywood story? "Virtue is its own reward." "Take off your glasses and you are beautiful." "Don't jump into the wrong bed and you'll marry rich."

The writer should ask himself what he is trying to say. Is it worth saying? Is it freshly said? Is it a significant statement that an audience will care about? Is it about life, death, love, or suicide, or is it simply about a character worrying about getting a date?

The conflict is the problem that the script is about

The story ends when the conflict is resolved. After the conflict is resolved, the shorter the final scene the better.

> After the villains are defeated in *Star Wars*, the only thing that is seen on the screen is the honoring of the heroes.

A Man for All Seasons is about the clash between Sir Thomas More and King Henry VIII. The screen goes dark when the axe falls on More's neck.

Locking the conflict

Conflict is the essence of narrative film. In the opening minutes of a film, two or more forces come into opposition. In film terms, the conflict is "locked" as quickly as possible. So urgent is the need to lock the conflict that many films do so in the tease before the title and credits.

In the opening frames of *High Noon*, the word reaches the sheriff that the bad men are returning to town. He decides he must remain to confront them. His decision affects everyone else in the film.

In *The Poseidon Adventure*, a cruise ship turns upside down, trapping many in the hull. Only when the trapped are freed or dead is the conflict resolved.

There is no drama until the sheriff decides to stay in town or until the ship overturns in a storm: until the conflict is locked.

Locking the conflict into a time frame heightens tension

The bomb will explode at six tonight.

Unless the carrier is found by two o'clock, the plague will spread.

Unless he is proven innocent by midnight, he will be executed.

The kidnappers will kill her unless they are paid by noon.

The terrorist will kill the hostages tonight unless his friends are escorted out of the country.

We must strengthen the dike before the flood takes it away.

The time lock adds suspense to the basic conflict by adding a fight against time.

Conflicts need not be locked by violent action

A man in a pea jacket walks to the end of a pier, spits into the water, and says he hates the sea.

A boy asks if anyone knows where his father can be found and gets only shrugs and sneers.

A girl in worn clothes stares at a "Help Wanted" sign.

Two men look at a mountain, and one of them says that a man could get killed up there.

Each of these opening scenes is enough to lock a conflict. The details of the conflict need not be stated the moment that the conflict is locked, but the viewer must know that there is a conflict and have some idea of its nature.

Kinds of conflict

① Conflict between a man and society:

The Grapes of Wrath
Julia
Odd Man Out

② Conflict between a man and himself:

Marty
Hamlet
Citizen Kane

③ Conflict between a man and another person:

The Sea Wolf
The Third Man
High Noon

④ Conflict between a man and nature:

Moby Dick
Track of the Cat
The Hurricane

Conflict is a form of action

Whether emotional or physical, conflict denotes action, a wrestling with the central problem at the core of a script, an effort—often fatal—to resolve the conflict. Conflict should be shown; it should not be told or explained.

>*Who's Afraid of Virginia Woolf?* opens with Martha and George screaming at each other.

>The ghost of Hamlet's father walks in Act I, Scene One.

>In *High Noon*, the man waiting for the released prisoners to arrive and confront the sheriff is seen in the opening, as are the clock and the railroad tracks, which become symbols of the conflict.

If the conflict is purely intellectual, it may be fascinating, as in *My Dinner with Andre*, but it will lack drama or action. If the conflict can be resolved by the dialogue alone, it certainly will not be visual. Used alone, conflict between two ideas, or two different views of the same idea, does not make for narrative film.

Action does not preclude expression of moral and intellectual issues

A film that couples action with moral or intellectual conflict allows for dramatic expression of the conflict. *High Noon* had two conflicts:

>The conflict with the outlaws that was resolved in a classic shoot-out.

>The different views of the importance of the civilizing factor—"The Tin Star" (the original title of the film and the story from which it was adapted; the title was later used for a different film).

The thematic climax was reached when the sheriff threw his badge in the dirt at the feet of the townspeople who had degraded that badge. Many people have read symbols of the McCarthy witch hunt period into this film. The fact that the film was a Western did not preclude expression of moral and intellectual issues.

The central conflict should be explored in depth from many points of view

The problems of the family in *A Long Day's Journey into Night*, a tale in which a father, mother, and two sons are in total conflict, are seen differently by each member of the family. Each has his or her own problems. The complexity of ways in which they can be viewed is vast.

The decision of the sheriff in *High Noon* to remain in town affects each person who comes on the screen: his wife, his former mistress, his friends, his clergyman, the judge, the deputy, etc.

In *Hamlet*, the conflict is seen from many points of view: through the eyes of Hamlet, his mother, his uncle, his friend Horatio, his fiancée, her father, and her brother.

Domestic conflict is the most universal of conflicts

Viewers have all been party to family conflict and they develop a Peeping-Tom relationship to the characters in *Who's Afraid of Virginia Woolf?*, *Ordinary People*, *Kramer vs Kramer*, or *Hamlet*. The viewer, looking at someone else's bared soul, is drawn into that character's problems and is emotionally involved with them. The best drama—from *Oedipus Rex* to *Hamlet* to *Who's Afraid of Virginia Woolf?* to *Death of a Salesman* to *A Long Day's Journey into Night* to *A Streetcar Named Desire*—has been the drama of family scandals. Tragic action is often not enemy against enemy, or among neutrals, but among friends or family.

Primal conflict—family conflict—is the stuff of high drama.

Hamlet's uncle murders his brother and marries his sister-in-law.

Oedipus kills his father and marries his mother.

Blanche du Bois (*A Streetcar Named Desire*) is raped by her brother-in-law and goes mad.

The problem of the scriptwriter is to understand how and when to draw back to keep this kind of tale from becoming melodrama or soap opera. The line between classic film or drama and melodrama or soap opera is fine. The difference lies in craftsmanship, restraint, understanding of moral implications, and understanding of the characters, as well as in the universality of the characters and their problems.

Violent conflicts make for good scripts

Violence does not necessarily mean physical violence, although it certainly may be. *Hamlet, High Noon, Oedipus Rex,* and *The Wild Bunch* are all physically violent dramas—but much more as well. But not all screen violence requires violent death or physical pain. Long-term and equally damaging pain can be caused by emotional violence.

In *Who's Afraid of Virginia Woolf?*, George murders Martha's imaginary child.

In *The Heiress*, Dr. Sloper emotionally destroys his daughter.

In *A Long Day's Journey into Night,* each of the characters is emotionally scarred for life by the actions or inactions of the others.

Emotional violence is often more readily understood by viewers than physical violence because of their kinship to it. Few people viewing a film have been shot, tortured, or run off a cliff in an automobile. Most people, however, are part of families and know the context of intimate family conflict, have been part of it, and understand its pain.

We enjoy violence because we are violent. However, in using violence, the writer must be careful not to move so fast that the audience cannot follow. The audience needs time to slow down and recover after violent scenes.

Conflict in drama is not necessarily violent

While violence makes for good scripts, a script need not be violent, not even emotionally violent, to work.

The failure of the father and daughter to understand each other in *On Golden Pond.*

The inability of the mother to accept her situation in *Ordinary People*.

The inability of *Marty*, an ugly, 36-year-old butcher, to get a date.

The confrontation and competition between generations in *All About Eve*.

These are not violent conflicts and they are not resolved by violence; they are emotional conflicts with which the viewer can identify and empathize.

Conflict does not preclude happiness on the screen; however, a conflict must be present in the background

Quiet scenes must have a conflict hanging over them. The viewer need not be clubbed over the head with the problems; the problems need only be foreshadowed. The viewer must be aware at all times that the happy characters are involved in an unresolved conflict that may keep them apart or kill them or destroy their plans for the future. Perhaps he is a hunted criminal or she is married, or she has a child out of wedlock. The problems may be family antipathy, illness, a criminal past, a draft card in his pocket, etc.

In *Love Is a Many Splendored Thing*, the fact that the heroine had an Oriental face and the hero a Caucasian one said all that was needed about their problem.

Consider, for example, a scene in which a man walks down a residential streeet, looks about, walks into the house, and calls his wife. She joins him, and he tells her he wants to go for a vacation. She thinks the idea is wonderful: When does he want to go? He says at once, and, laughingly, they start packing. This is basically a dull scene. Put it aside.

A car drives down the same residential street. The driver is looking for an address. He sees it, pulls over to the curb, takes a revolver out of the glove compartment, checks the clip to make certain there are bullets in the chamber, cocks the revolver, and, making a U-turn, parks across the street from the house.

Now, run the first piece of film. That previously dull scene now has a conflict behind it that changes the entire effect of the original scene, although not a frame has been changed. The viewer must always be aware of the potential for conflict behind a quiet scene.

Conflict changes the protagonist

The Aristotelian theory that the conflict must be large enough to change the central character remains valid in the film script. If the problem is not important enough to change the character, the viewers' reasons for watching it have been removed.

In *High Noon*, the clear indication that the sheriff has changed takes place after the climax, when he is asked to remain in the town as sheriff. He throws the badge for which he risked his marriage and his life in the dust at the feet of the townspeople, indicating his clear change of character as a result of the conflict.

At the end of *Casablanca*, Rick, who has remained aloof from the war, walks off to join the French Resistance.

Size and significance of the conflict

The Aristotelian concept of appropriate size is related to the size and significance of the conflict. No one would try to make an *I Love Lucy* episode the same length as *War and Peace;* the conflict in the former would not sustain the drama. Nor would one try to make *War and Peace* in a half hour; the conflict is too large for the time allowed. The size of the conflict is determined by different conditions.

If a character such as Howard Hughes loses a hundred dollars, that would not pose a significant problem. But a poor delivery man may lose his bicycle and, by that, his job and his ability to care for his family. From this problem, DeSica made *The Bicycle Thief.*

An 18-year-old fraternity boy may find failing to get a date for the prom a problem; the viewer rarely does. But if a 36-year-old butcher who thinks himself ugly fails to get a date week after week, the story may be *Marty*. The 18-year-old will get a date another day; the 36-year-old might never.

The conflict can be outside the control of the characters

The source of conflict can be a war, a sinking ship, or a storm. However, the character must be deeply involved in the war, as in *All Quiet on the Western Front;* the sinking ship, as in *The Poseidon Adventure;* or the storm, as in *The Hurricane.*

The moral dimension of a conflict greatly enhances the viewer's involvement

In *The Professionals*, writer-director Richard Brooks complicated the moral problem by having his heroes accept a firm moral commitment to seek out and possibly destroy a man who turns out to have been an old comrade-in-arms. The complexity of the moral problem and how the characters coped with this conflict within themselves, apart from their mission, gave the film a dimension beyond that of most Westerns.

The moral conflict in *The Ox-Bow Incident* raised the simple Western lynching tale to artistic heights and gave it the tone of a medieval morality play.

If the hero and heroine are not involved in the conflict, those about them must be

Romeo and Juliet have families in conflict.

The Eurasian heroine of *Love Is a Many Splendored Thing* is not involved in the conflict by anything she says or does: racial difference is the conflict.

The conflict must bring the antagonist and protagonist together

These are the persons in conflict and they must resolve it one way or another. A confrontation between the antagonist and protagonist is considered to be an "obligatory scene."

The climax of *The Wind and the Lion* suffered because the bedouin chief in Morocco and President Theodore Roosevelt in Washington, D.C., were unable to confront each other at any time in the film.

An unresolved conflict leaves the viewer unsatisfied

The viewer has been watching to see how the conflict will be resolved. He may not like an unhappy resolution, but he will like it considerably more than no resolution.

In *Hud*—which was originally written with the nephew as the central character—Hud has alienated the woman he loves, failed to make peace with his dying father, and, finally, alienated his nephew who loves him. Hud's reaction to his final total isolation from family and friends is a gesture that indicates he does not care. If a man can have so many negative things happen to him because of what he has done or failed to do, he must be emotionally crippled. The viewer feels only pity for Hud and is unsatisfied, as there is no resolution to the problem, which actually is an unchanged protagonist.

CHAPTER 3

═══

Structure

"Writing for the screen has nothing to do with mechanics and everything to do with character, story, and structure. Structure, structure, structure."

—RICHARD BROOKS

Plot elements

Plot is the frame upon which the basic idea of the script is hung, the substructure of the whole.

Plot is structure. It is the most difficult part of scriptwriting. The crises selected in or selected out determine the quality of the script. A crisis in the wrong place, or a crisis needed but not present, can destroy a script.

The plot is made up of scenes, incidents, and crises, which are organized to develop the conflict from the moment it is locked through its complex parts to the resolution of the conflict. The order and selection of the scenes determines the plot and creates the structure of the script.

Climax and resolution. The script is written with the climax in mind. The writer should first select his conflict, then figure out its climax and resolution. The middle—everything else—can be filled in last.

The master scene. All action and dialogue that takes place within one setting is considered a master scene. Plot, character, dialogue, exposition, and structure are the responsibility of the writer; *how* these elements are placed on the screen is the responsibility of the director. The script tells the director what the writer wants on the screen—not how to get it there. For that reason, the master scene has taken over in scriptwriting. The writer does not break the scene down into individual shots. The director, the production manager, and the editor determine how many ways and times a scene will be shot or reshot.

Length of script and number and length of scenes. A 100-minute-long feature film averages twenty-four to twenty-six different scenes or crises. These will average five pages each. The finished script averages slightly less than a page a minute when filmed. A 120-page script will generally yield a hundred minutes of finished film. The art of the screenplay is in the selection and ordering of these twenty-four to twenty-six scenes. This does not mean all films are or should be 100 minutes. It only means that 100-minute films allow for audience turnover in a theater and fit in two-hour time slots for commercial television viewing.

Scenes are complete in themselves. They have their own structure: a beginning, a middle, and an end. They begin at a particular moment and usually contain a crisis or confrontation. Scenes are created by bringing different characters together at different stages of the conflict.

Selection and ordering of scenes. A conflict is made up of a series of crises, straining points in the conflict that cause a realignment of forces or some change in the character. The plot is created by the selection and ordering of these crises. In each scene's internal crisis, an action is taken or not taken, or a decision is made or not made knowingly by the characters.

> Hamlet knowingly does not kill his uncle at prayer. He knowingly kills his uncle after being poisoned.

Crises are moments of tension all relating to the central conflict.

17

Different scenes may construct the same plot. A different *order* of incidents probably will change the plot.

> A woman is murdered. Her husband is arrested and charged. His girlfriend finds proof of his guilt but helps him through the trial. He is acquitted. They leave for the Bahamas.

> A woman is murdered. Her husband is arrested and charged. His girlfriend helps him through the trial. He is acquitted. They leave for the Bahamas. There she finds proof of his guilt.

In the first version the girlfriend is a guilty accomplice; in the second, an innocent victim. The difference is entirely in the placement of the one scene: her discovery of his guilt. All other scenes can be in the identical order, and yet the plot, the tension points, and the moral choices all create a different film. The rearrangement or replacement of one or two scenes can substantially alter the plot.

Particular scenes in a particular order create a singular script. Changing these elements creates a different film.

The action in which confrontations take place is the plot.

> Hamlet confronts his mother, his uncle, Laertes, and Ophelia.

> Sheriff Will Kane confronts or is confronted by his wife, mistress, the judge, his friend, and the townspeople.

> Luke Skywalker confronts each of his future companions as well as his enemies.

Causality and integration. Aristotle said it is the synthesis of incidents that gives form to the play as a whole. A plot is a series of roughly twenty-five scenes, each related to the next, each knitting and unraveling the threads of the plot. If one scene does not cause the next, all you have is a series of tableaux.

> A plot is also a narrative of events, the emphasis falling on causality. "The king died and then the queen died" is a story. "The king died, and then the queen died of grief" is a plot. The time-sequence is preserved, but the sense of causality overshadows it.
> —E. M. Forster, *Aspects of the Novel*

Had he been writing about film rather than the novel, he might have added, "and because the queen died there was no heir, and because there was no heir there was chaos in the kingdom."

Relationships develop from scene to scene. A frequently heard criticism if the relationships are incidental or coincidental and not causally related is that a script is contrived. One action or idea should relate to another and cause it to happen or prevent it from happening.

> Hamlet's father dies. Prodded by his father's ghost, Hamlet's desire to learn how his father died becomes obsessive, and because of this his fiancée kills herself and Hamlet confronts his mother and kills Polonius, his fiancée's father, and because of this his fiancée's brother becomes his enemy, etc.

Because Hamlet's father died and the ghost walked, each incident that followed was related to or caused by the ghost's charge to Hamlet.

> Will Kane, the sheriff in *High Noon*, hears the outlaws are returning to the town and he decides to remain and protect the town.

Because of Kane's decision, his wife leaves him, the townspeople turn against him, the judge flees, and Kane's former mistress flees.

Scene is saddled to scene by causal relationship. Causality helps construct a plot.

Reversal, discovery, and recognition. Reversal means a change from one situation to its opposite: good fortune to bad or vice versa. In reversal, the action swings to the opposite direction, but still in accord with the laws of probability.

> In *Oedipus Rex*, the servant-messenger comes to cheer Oedipus by letting him know who his mother really is, and in so doing achieves just the opposite. Oedipus is plunged into misery.

In a discovery or recognition scene, those marked for good or bad fortune pass from ignorance to knowledge, revealing love or hate, resulting in either friendships or enmities. Recognition or discovery may be accompanied by reversal.

19

Plots are simple or complex. In a simple plot, a change of fortune occurs without a reversal or recognition scene.

In the film *Wuthering Heights*, Heathcliff overhears only part of a conversation in which Catherine tells her maid that she could never marry Heathcliff. Because of this discovery, Heathcliff flees without hearing the end of Catherine's speech, in which she says that she will always love Heathcliff and he will always be a part of her.

There is no actual reversal in the feelings of the two lovers, nor in their fate: the two will still love each other until and even after death. They have not been thwarted from marrying; they could never have married even if Heathcliff had stayed. A change of fortune occurred to each of them: Catherine married a man she disliked, and Heathcliff became a wealthy gentleman.

A complex plot is one in which the change of fortune is brought about by a reversal or recognition scene or both. In every plot, the "how" of discovery is the action.

The crisis may be emotional or physical; it should not be intellectual. The well-made screenplay is all plot—suspense, tempo, intrigue, and, above all, action—but without emotion, it becomes pure mechanical contrivance. The selection and organization of the scenes in the best possible ascending order toward a climax must evoke emotional reactions in the characters and in the audience. If the viewer doesn't care what happens, he will be bored. What reactions will a scene evoke? Wonder? Awe? Fear? Pleasure? Hate? Or boredom?

The film *Rollover* was a colossal bore and failure because the plot was limited to the intricacies of financial maneuverings and was too esoteric to engage a general audience emotionally.

Plot is more than a pattern of events: it is the ordering of emotions. If the plot is all action and little emotion, it is melodrama.

Rambo: First Blood II, although a popular and financial success, merely exploited the audience taste for gratuitous violence; it is melodrama.

Suspense and astonishment. The possibility of coming crises should be foreshadowed. Viewers want to know if things prophesied will come true. A good plot is structured to keep the viewer wanting to know what is going to happen next and if or how the conflict will be resolved. Coming doom is more impressive by a gradual inevitability than by a sudden fall.

If Sherlock Holmes solves the crime in the first ten minutes, there is no reason to keep watching.

If the viewer knows who will and who will not survive in *The Great Escape*, there will no longer be any reason to watch.

Humans revel in mishaps and disasters to others. A story strings together the imitation of these events. Given incident A, the audience wants to know incident B. Astonish the audience with A and they will feel the suspense of wanting to know B. Two ingredients of suspense in narrative are crude action and astonishment.

Epiphany. The quality in drama or film known as epiphany is the sudden manifestation, the really meaningful moment that startles the viewer even as he recognizes that it is right. It is unexpected, but totally logical within its context.

In *Terms of Endearment*, when the daughter (Debra Winger) tells her mother (Shirley MacLaine) that she is going to become a grandmother, a viewer might expect a reaction of joy. Instead, MacLaine starts to scream that she doesn't want to be a grandmother.

The famous half-grapefruit in the face scene in *Public Enemy* is totally unexpected and implausible in any context other than the relationship between Cagney's character and that played by Mae Clark.

In the opening of *Slither*, two men enter a house. Without warning, they are shot at and one is shoved down the cellar steps. He continues to hear gunfire, pokes his head up through the trap-door, and sees his companion sitting in an easy chair, smoking, a stack of dynamite about to explode at his side.

The unexpected, the unanticipated is more refreshing and entertaining than the routine. Such moments are rare, but memorable. However, the unexpected can be overdone to the point where the viewer will no longer suspend disbelief. The line is a fine one and must be watched with care.

The familiar. The viewer is prepared to believe the familiar in a plot. Few intelligent people have not contemplated suicide as Hamlet does. Most viewers are aware of marriages like that of George and Martha in *Who's Afraid of Virginia Woolf?* Few viewers have not felt as lonely as Marty or known others who have. Few viewers have not known an estranged relationship with an aunt or uncle or parent as does the young hero of the *Star Wars* trilogy. These are the familiar aspects of conflict. (The setting, however, need not be familiar, as *Star Wars* proved.)

Different views. Each scene should give the audience different views of the story. A problem without many sides will be flat. Characters serve to bounce the problem off in different ways.

Each scene should advance the plot. If a scene can be removed without changing those that precede and follow it, something is wrong with the structure of the script. Each scene should carry information about one or more of the characters that the viewer must know in order to understand the next scene, or it must carry action, decision, or indecision that the viewer must be aware of in subsequent scenes.

If a scene does not move the narrative forward, does not complicate the conflict by tightening it, or does not begin to resolve the conflict, it should probably be eliminated. Buster Keaton removed what he considered to be one of his funniest sequences from *The General* because it stopped the onward flow of his story and therefore did not belong in the film. If the right scenes are in the right order, revisions, editing, and cutting should take place within the scenes.

Climax and resolution

Every scene, decision, or lack of it, creates and shapes the climax. Structure requires the organization of the selected scenes in the best possible ascending order toward a climax. The point of maximum strain is the climax, where everything is brought into focus and the conflict is resolved. The tension peaks and creates a new balance, and denouement follows.

An obligatory scene is the confrontation between the antagonist and the protagonist in which the conflict is resolved, as in the following climaxes:

Hamlet kills Claudius

George kills Martha's child that never existed

In *High Noon* the sheriff's wife kills the villain.

In *Casablanca* Ingrid Bergman goes off with her husband, leaving Humphrey Bogart.

Oedipus destroys himself.

Conflict resolution without confrontation tends to be weak and unsatisfying, as in *The Wind and the Lion.*

A climax that takes place inside the head of the central character lacks drama.

In *A Man and a Woman*, the heroine makes the crucial decision to change her mind and stay with the hero instead of breaking up with him while she is alone on a train. She discusses this with no one. The viewer only knows what she has decided to do when she rejoins him. This lonely ride was the turning point of the story. The climax that brought about a complete reversal of her actions took place in her head where the viewer cannot go. The photography was pretty; the dramatic action was bad.

Emotional violence is often more meaningful than physical violence, as in the climax of *Who's Afraid of Virginia Woolf?* when George kills Martha's child, committing a violent act of imaginary but emotional murder.

Talking out a problem is a poor visual or dramatic resolution. A "come to realize" speech is inadequate.

Guess Who's Coming to Dinner ended with the main characters sitting around the table discussing their new insights or changed attitudes to prejudice and tolerance. As a result, the ending lacked dramatic power.

Death is not necessarily a resolution.

In the film *Natural Enemies* the protagonist plans to kill his wife and children and himself. He tells his plan to three friends, each of whom tries to dissuade him. In the closing shot he shoots his wife and children and himself. The picture was a total failure despite a good cast and direction because the protagonist did not make a moral decision, did not solve the problems of his unhappiness, but evaded them.

The death of a villain in a Western by a heart attack or accident would not resolve the film's problem, which is a conflict between the hero and the villain, between good and evil.

The protagonist must solve the problem, choose and make the final moral decision.

The conflict and its resolution must change the character. The audience must understand that a change has taken place in the lead character, why the change took place, and what caused the change.

Denouement

The action that takes place after the conflict has been resolved is known as the denouement, falling action, or wrap-up. After the conflict is resolved in the climax, the film should end as quickly as possible. The only thing that should take place after the resolution of the conflict is a scene tying up any loose narrative ends that might leave the viewer unsatisfied.

Hamlet's death ends the narrative. All that is left for the viewer of Shakespeare's time was to learn what happened to the kingdom. Fortinbras, a relative and obvious heir to the throne, enters, and Hamlet is carried off to be buried.

In *A Man for All Seasons*, Sir Thomas More refused to sanction the king's divorce. After many attempts to change More's mind, the king orders More's execution. The film ended dramatically when the executioner's axe fell and the screen cut to black.

In *Little Big Man*, the highest point of action in the film was the last stand of Custer. Though there was no suspense, as the viewers all knew how this battle would end, there was the suspense that is always present when fictional characters are placed alongside historical characters: continuing interest in what is going to happen to the fictional characters. From the shot where Little Big Man is wounded and sits looking at the battlefield around him, the action is on a downward slope. The delightfully warm part of the story, in which his Indian father goes out to die and finds that the magic does not work, is not really high in drama and is certainly not telling the audience anything more than they have already learned.

In short, material followed the climax that did not need to follow it, a structural weakness in an otherwise good script. For the sake of dramatic structure, it would have been simple to place the scene with the old Indian *before* the Custer battle and to cut from Little Big Man wounded on the battlefield to the old man talking to the young researcher in the home for the aged. In this way, the falling action would have been shortened and nothing would have been lost.

In a television drama of one or two hours, there is often a beginning, a middle, and an end, and a separate episode after the commercial, sometimes called an epilogue or a tag, for a denouement.

Unity of theme, time, place, style

Unity of theme. The writer's basic responsibility is unity and arrangement. A film is an organic whole; if the viewer loses sight of one aspect because of another, something is wrong. In a tightly unified script, every action should be related to the central conflict, the theme. Every action need not be related to the protagonist, but it must be related to the central premise. Unity of conflict is necessary. All subplots must relate to the main problem.

If something can be cut out of a script without the viewer being aware of it at the end, it wasn't part of the organic whole.

In *High Noon*, every action follows logically from the sheriff's decision to remain in the town and confront the bad men. There is nothing in the film that does not relate to this decision.

In the opening scene of *Marty* are the lines, "I hear your brother is getting married. When are you gonna get married, Marty?" In Marty's climactic speech, he says he is going to call the girl, ask her for a date, and get down on his knees and ask her to marry him. Everything in between relates to the opening question.

Unity of time. A story can be told vertically (events happen in chronological order), or it can be told horizontally (events happen all at the same time in different locations as in *The Longest Day*, *Grand Hotel*, or *The Hospital*).

Aristotle's concept of unity of time held the length of the drama to the time of one day. Few film stories take place in their own actual time structure. The exceptions have been *Rope*, *The Set-Up*, and *High Noon*.

In modern drama, the fight against time becomes important, even if it takes years. The "clock" is movie shorthand for the deadline toward which villains push their plans and against which the hero struggles. A built-in time lock insures suspense:

The bomb due to go off in two hours.

The girl is going to die unless . . .

Five days to accomplish the mission, or . . .

Two Minute Warning is an example of the clock running.

A story can start at a natural time and end at a natural time; that is, it can start with a war beginning and end with the war ending. However, the action in between does not have to take place in its actual, natural time.

Unity of time has dominated much modern film, almost eliminating the film that spans extended periods. For example, the novel *Six Days of the Condor* became the film *Three Days of the Condor.* An epic story has the inherent problem that it is hard to lock together scenes with years between them.

Unity of place. A locale can create unity: *The Towering Inferno, Grand Hotel, Airport.* However, beware false unity: *Ship of Fools* failed because of its structure. The various characters on the ship were not related; there was unity of place but no unity of theme.

Unity of style. The writer's style and vision, be it mythic, realistic, or Hollywood romantic, is a large part of the unity of the film. The moment that unity is broken, the audience is lost. How does the writer approach his material? Poetically, with the use of a poetic phrase and a poetic eye that sees images instead of solid character, symbols instead of people? Or brutally realistic, so that the viewer is able to say, "Yes, this is the way things are, this is the way people act, this set looks as though people walked these streets, slept in these beds, and copulated, and begat between these sheets"? Or is it all as in a James Bond film, a mythic world we would like to believe really does exist?

The way the writer approaches his material is his style: the vision he has of the story. Almost any story might have more than one vision, but when one has been selected, it must be consistent throughout.

The viewer is prepared to accept almost anything in a story if it is true in its context. That "willing suspension of disbelief for the moment, which constitutes poetic faith," as

27

Coleridge said, allows the writer to create *Star Wars, Journey to the Center of the Earth, Superman, E.T.,* and even to expect applause when asking in *Peter Pan,* "Do you believe in fairies?" In addition, it allows the writer to write of heroes and heroic deeds.

However, Coleridge's "for the moment" is a clear warning that the context cannot be changed from realism to fantasy without a jolt to the viewer's willingness to suspend his disbelief. A film cannot go from science fiction, which suspends disbelief, to contemporary realism without suffering a loss of that element of poetic faith. (This is not to say that a science fiction film, for example, must eschew anything realistic.) The *Star Wars* trilogy is true to itself. *The Exorcist* was true to itself. The same is true of any film that holds its viewers.

The fictional documentary-style feature creates its own illusion of reality. *13 Rue Madeleine, Boomerang, The House on 92nd Street, To the Ends of the Earth,* and *The Naked City* all used specific times, actual places, and narrators to create the illusion that the fictional story being told was a real story that took place with real people in a particular time. A post–World War II technique, this is different from what has been called docu-drama, which attempts to re-create reality, as was done in *Battle of Algiers.*

The French Connection and *Serpico,* more recent film adaptations of books based on true stories, did not attempt the effect of reality that is used in fictional documentary, but relied on straightforward storytelling.

Miscellaneous structural techniques and problems

Time lapse. To create the illusion of time passing, the viewer's attention must be diverted twice. The hero asks a friend to drive to his home three to five miles away and return with a pie. The hero then asks someone else to fetch a cup of coffee. The phone rings and the hero speaks for one minute or less. If the friend then returns with the pie, the viewers will be aware that in real time he could not have driven three to five miles, fetched a pie, and returned. The request for a cup of coffee and the phone call are enough to create the dramatic time lapse.

Flashbacks. Flashbacks must be an integral part of the structure, not a technique of exposition. Dramatic flashbacks as exposition to present one, **two,** or three pieces of information are awkward. They slow a narrative rather than move it forward and the viewer becomes aware of the technique.

In the novel *The Entity*, there is a flashback **to** reveal Carlotta's memories of her earlier life. For the film adaptation, a flashback at the same moment, prior to a supernatural attack, would have destroyed the suspense. The information from the novel's flashback was included in normal exposition and dialogue.

Properly used, the flashback organizes the storyline.

The flashbacks in *Citizen Kane, All About Eve,* and *A Letter to Three Wives* are structural. The writer selected a time in the present, flashed back to one or more times in the past, brought the story back one or more times to the present, and then passed through the present to the climax of the story. *Two for the Road* and *Slaughterhouse Five* had similar structures.

The science fiction comedy *Back to the Future* introduced a clever twist on the structural use of the flashback. The film opened in the present and flashed back to a time before the protagonist's birth, taking him back in time for an encounter with his own parents as youngsters. At the end, he is returned to the present, but finds that what he did while "back there" affected the lives of all involved. He finds his family very much changed. (See *Unity of time.*)

The writer may suggest a transition method for the flashback —e.g., he may specify *soft-focus.*

A plant. Any prop that will be used in the plot should be planted with care in the story or visual. Examples:

A man under threat grabs a fireplace iron.

A man running down a street suddenly turns and fires a revolver.

A woman about to be raped draws a switchblade knife from her purse.

A lawyer takes a fully drawn contract from his pocket.

A driver whose car is out of gas in an empty desert takes out a jerry can filled with gasoline.

The chase scene. The chase has become a cliché. The horse chase, car chase, etc., have become routine. Only the unusual chase, as in *The French Connection,* will attract attention. Television uses a dozen car chases a week. These differ in no particular way: corners are turned, brakes screech, cars rolled over or are smashed, dead-ends are reached. The scriptwriter who adds something new to his chase scene, if he feels he *must* have a chase, separates his script from the others.

Biography. Film biographies tend to cover only a segment of a person's life—*Sunrise at Campobello* treated one part of Franklin Delano Roosevelt's life, *Gandhi* one part of Mohandas Gandhi's life, and *Coal Miner's Daugher* one part of singer Loretta Lynn's life. It is difficult to sustain unity and interest over the larger time frame of an entire life.

Biography presents special problems: The subject, if living, must give permission, and family permission must also be obtained; if the subject is dead, family permission is still needed. There has been no biographical film about Charlie Chaplin because the family will not give permission. There are some notable exceptions:

Are You Now or Have You Ever Been?, which was about the investigation of Communist activity in Hollywood, did not require permission because the hearing transcripts, which were a matter of public record, were used word for word.

All the President's Men, which dealt with the breaking of the Watergate story, required permission only from the reporters; the other characters were public figures and elected officials from whom no permission was needed.

For the film *Patton,* about the military career of General George Patton, permission was given on condition that the family never appear or be mentioned in the script.

Researching the subject of the story. If the story background or scientific, geographic, historic, or biographic details are unfamiliar to the writer, they should be researched, whether on location, in interviews, or in the library. *Important:* When you start to write the script, put away the books and notes. You'll remember what is dramatically significant and you'll avoid cluttering up the script with irrelevant facts.

Historical accuracy is not always a necessity in theatrical film. Most viewers will reject a film in which a Lincoln or John Kennedy dies of old age. However, few viewers knew anything about Butch Cassidy and the Sundance Kid. Few knew anything about the death of Mussolini or the Battle of Tobruk. Theatrical film has an obligation to entertain, and if the facts get in the way of the story, the writer can change them, even if that is altering history. Theatrical film has little obligation to educate with facts. The number of historical details changed in the making of *Gandhi,* for example, would fill a historical study. Certainly, it is better that details be correct whenever possible, but the film may be seen by millions and only a few viewers may be offended by changes in historical detail.

Transition from person to the same person. Most viewers find jump cuts from a character in one place to the same character in another place disorienting. If it is necessary to cut from person to the same person, invent a fresh way of doing so. In *I Never Sang for My Father,* sound covered the transition from one scene to the next.

Violence may be a necessity within the context of a particular plot and between characters. Eric Bentley rightly said, "To grab an audience, use violence. To hold an audience, use more violence. A good play is more than violence but it need not eschew it."

The conflict in *Hamlet* can be resolved only by violence. At the end, all of the principal characters are dead.

High Noon could only be resolved by a violent confrontation between good and evil.

Violence and death that are well motivated, consistent within the context of the plot, and move the conflict toward its resolution are generally acceptable. The carnage of *Apocalypse Now* was never criticized.

Avoid coincidence in plot. Two people saying the same thing, for example. It's a cheap, undramatic technique.

When somebody criticizes a story as "contrived," they usually mean there is too much coincidence. Contrived, meaning created with forethought and planning, is frequently used as a pejorative term when applied to a script. When so used, the chances are that the plot is too mechanical, the characters too lacking in dimension, or the coincidences too unlikely (*deus ex machina*). All plots are contrived, but they must not appear to be so. Shakespeare's plots are so good because the contrivance is invisible.

Overheard, unexposed scenes are clumsy dramatic "devices." The scene in which the villain and villainess are overheard speaking the truth or revealing a scheme by the last person whom he or she wants to know this information is an embarrassingly awkward cliché.

A story hole is an unexplained piece of story. Examples:

When Elmer Gantry leaves a moving railroad car at the opening of the film by that name, he is without his suitcase or his shoes. In the next shot he enters a store carrying a vacuum cleaner he is trying to sell. Where did it come from?

In *The Appaloosa* the character played by Marlon Brando is told he cannot get into town. Later, when he is wounded, the audience hears that he cannot get out of town. In the next shot, he is out of town.

In *In the Heat of the Night* there is no explanation of how the detective, played by Sidney Poitier, came to know the old woman who held the key to the solution of the crime.

Such lapses in story design shatter the willing suspension of disbelief and leave the audience unsatisfied.

Symbolism should be used with a clear-cut purpose. Muddied symbols indicate lack of clear thought. Avoid such clichés as:

> The character dressed to represent evil or death.
>
> The Jew who is beaten and falls to lie with his arms outstretched to look like another Jew on a cross.
>
> The cut from a fierce man's face to an eagle.

Beware also such overdone symbols as:

> The horses in heat neighing to suggest seduction, as in *Not as a Stranger*.
>
> The flower crushed underfoot to indicate a rape, as in *Gone to Earth* (the American version was *The Wild Heart*).
>
> The birds wheeling overhead to represent the conflict in the house in *The Trojan Women*.

Weather should not be described unless integral to the story. It is hard—and expensive—to invent.

Probability, plausibility, and chance. The plausible is more important than what can be demonstrated as probable or possible. In an ongoing film there is no time for the audience to evaluate the chances for or against something happening. If it seems at all plausible, the audience will accept it. If it seems *incredible* on the face of it, no logic or evidence will prevail.

> That a whole defensive regiment of French soldiers could flee their trenches because of a collective supernatural vision would seem incredible to most audiences, even though it did, in fact, occur during World War I.
>
> That an unstable foreign government could paralyze American foreign policy for a year by kidnapping fifty-two hostages would have been incredible to audiences before the Ayatollah Khomeini did it.

The writer should not argue with the viewer, or cause the viewer to argue with him. An audience will accept paste jewels, phony backdrops, but an improbable incident does not make good drama. The *fact* of it does not matter. The audience is entitled to plausibility of theme, character, and development.

Drama is not life, but an imitation of life; an imitation not of men as such, but of action and life, of happiness and misery, not as states of being but as forms of activity. Men are good, bad, happy, or sad in the things they do, or, as in Hamlet's case, are unable to do.

CHAPTER 4

▬

Character

"What is character but the determination of incident? What is incident but the illustration of character?"
—HENRY JAMES

A character in a film is a representation of a person exhibiting certain personality traits selected for a dramatic purpose.

Function and definition

Characters are not just faces talking. The viewer needs to know several aspects of the main characters: physical, mental, cultural, and moral. The viewer needs to know why a character acts as he does—his motivation. There must be a logical inevitability to his actions. What he does may be surprising, but when considered, it must make sense, it must be rational. Thus, psychopathic characters have limited dramatic value. Psychopaths are irrational; they can do anything without established motivation. Most viewers feel a limited empathy to such characters. The audience much prefers to understand a character, relate to him, feel for him, and root for him. Why else watch the film?

Relationship of character and plot

Aristotle said that men are certain kinds of individuals as a result of their characters, but they become happy or miserable a a result of their actions. Thus, drama is not a portrayal of character, but of action; the soul of drama is the plot. The plot is more important than the characters. Therefore, dramatists do not employ action to achieve character portrayal, they include characters because of their relations to action.

A character is revealed by what he does. A character can describe himself, or others can speak of his many positive qualities, his kindness, his generosity, his spirituality, but if the viewer sees him shoving his grandmother down a flight of steps in her wheelchair, that action determines his character. Nothing said about a character has any significance in the viewer's understanding of him if it is different from what the viewer has seen. The character is understood in the context of his actions.

One of our greatest modern creators of character, Paddy Chayefsky, wrote, "In drama, you create a set of incidents and you develop characters to execute those incidents. The characters take shape in order to make the story true . . . as a rule, your character has to be capable of performing the incidents required by the story."

A character is developed in relation to other characters; he must act upon, react to, and, in turn, be acted upon by others. He is revealed by encounter, decision, action, and reaction.

In the film industry, the lead character is very important; producers will ask about the character before the story because of the star factor in financing and distribution. And film critics tend to praise character portrayal more than plot because the audience identifies with the characters. This is not the natural way to work on a screenplay, and it creates distortions.

What characters does the plot need?

The most essential character is the protagonist, the hero, or often today, the anti-hero. In classical drama, the protagonist performed noble deeds; he was morally good and chose good over evil. Today's protagonist is often a man who stands against society and its standards rather than one who defends them. This man is less a hero than a central figure who is not heroic, but human. The hero still has a place. When he is all-powerful, he is Batman or Superman; when he is flawed, he is Willy Loman in *Death of a Salesman.* If the flaws dominate, he is an anti-hero.

The second character needed is the one with whom the hero is involved. There could be no Hamlet without Claudius, no Othello without Desdemona; they "play off" each other. This second character need not be the villain or the antagonist in the conflict. (Romeo would not have been possible without Juliet.) But, if the second character is the antagonist, he must be strong, because it is against him that the hero is measured. There is no heroism in vanquishing a weakling or a fool.

If the German defenders in *The Guns of Navarone* were known in advance to be underage conscripts, poorly armed, the Allied commandoes would have been robbed of their heroic stature in overcoming them.

The villain should not be all bad, nor the hero perfect; characters should be shaded. The audience must know enough about them to understand them and believe that they would act the way they do.

The third necessary character is the one who helps bring about the climax:

Polonius in *Hamlet.*

Cassio in *Othello.*

The Amish boy in *Witness* who initiates the action by witnessing a murder, identifies the corrupt policeman, and finally rings the bell to bring in the other Amish in time to save the hero's life.

The third character may have a small role but he is the one who makes the proposition important, such as the Ghost in *Hamlet* or the Goatherd in *Oedipus Rex.*

For film, minor characters need not be fully developed; they can be flat. They need not change as the protagonist must. Television serial drama is the opposite: The lead character tends to remain static from week to week, while the minor characters are developed and changed.

People can be used as props. A scene filled with extras

brings the scene to life. Few people walk down empty streets; in film, public places should be populated.

Qualities, traits, and idiosyncrasies of characters

Aristotle said, "A character is a collection of qualities." The writer must know much more about his characters than will be used in the film. It may be worthwhile to write biographical sketches of the main characters, describing family background, motivations, attitudes, social status, occupation, hobbies, education, religion, marital status, race, and ethnic origins. Any or all of these may affect the character's behavior. Is he fat or thin? Ugly or handsome? Young or old? Neat or sloppy? Personality, temperament, and intellectual capacity are all the responsibility of the writer. Obviously, these qualities must be varied in the different characters.

Speech habits distinguish characters. Speech habits reveal attitudes toward sex, race, religion, and politics. Is a character terse? Long-winded? Does he stammer? Drawl? Repeat certain words or phrases? Does he have a foreign or regional accent?

Character is revealed in conflict. The writer's choice of twenty-four or twenty-five scenes, crises, decision points, or confrontations make the character. If the character responds to everything in the same way without changing, he may be dramatically poor. This is not a problem for the comic character, who doesn't change, who repeats old responses to situations; he or she is often more of a stereotype than a character: the long-suffering mother, the lantern-jawed hero, the mother-in-law, the girl next door. But the main characters must reveal themselves in their actions.

Characters are best revealed by their fury against each other, against nature, against society. The stuff of drama is the character who does not react exactly as expected. He should hold surprises for the audience, but he must be believable. The audience doesn't want to waste time psychoanalyzing the character; they want to see him in action. They want to see him work out his destiny and change. A character comes to a logical solution to his problem, a solution another character would not come to, according to the characteristics the writer gives him.

Development and change. In order to be credible, the main character must develop and change in some way because of what has happened to him. As the story develops, further revelations of character disclose aspects of the character the audience did not know previously. However, latent, new, unexpected qualities should be foreshadowed; sudden change is not believable.

At the same time, the change must be dramatic and the audience must be made aware of it. It is not enough for the character to say, "And I came to realize . . ."

The sheriff in *High Noon* demonstrates his integrity, loyalty, and courage throughout. It is only at the end, when he tosses his badge in the dirt and leaves town, that the audience becomes aware of the change brought about in the man by the conflict and feels perhaps a momentary surprise. But his action is believable in the context of the story and the character's earlier behavior.

The heroine of *Gaslight* is manipulated by her husband toward insanity. Yet, in the happy ending, there is no flat "came to realize" speech; instead, she traps him in his foul scheme. Her "recovery" is believable because the audience knows that her insanity had been artificially induced by her husband.

Fleshing out a character. Small touches, small actions, or small gestures round out a character. The scene in *Lawrence of Arabia* in which Lawrence lights a match and deliberately burns himself revealed an important aspect of his character better than words could have.

The courage of a character need not be physical courage. It can be shown by risking a job, testifying for a friend, etc.

Self-image as revelation of character and motivation. The revelation of character takes place on several levels. The most important is the level of actions and decisions. However, the character's concept of himself is also important in explaining his personality, motivations, and actions. If, at some point in the film, possibly in no more than a few lines, the character can tell how he sees himself in relation to the conflict, the audience can achieve a better understanding of the character. It is not important that his view be the actual truth—the viewer sees that truth through the actions of the character— but it must be the truth as the character has explained those actions to himself. The character's truth may be his motivation.

In *Apocalypse Now*, the personal philosophy and disgust with war and violence expressed at the beginning, with the recruitment of the special agent (Martin Sheen) assigned to finding and killing the rogue officer (Marlon Brando), explains the agent's eventual breakdown and retreat from the horrors of the Vietnam War.

In the film of *Elmer Gantry*, the preacher describes himself in his sermons as the messenger of God and shepherd of the flock, motivated by godly love. That others see him as a charlatan penetrates his consciousness only slowly.

A character may be insane, but his motives must be rational from his point of view. It should be clear to the viewer why the character thinks he does what he does.

The character and his motivations are revealed by the decisions he does or does not make. He is one kind of person if he takes a risk to help a friend, a different kind if he does or does not take a risk to help a stranger. He may steal because he must; he may steal because it is his way of life; or he may decide to starve rather than steal.

It is hard to figure out the motivations of real people. With fictional characters, the writer must create their motivations; he must invent the reasons why the character acts the way he does. Sex, ambition, and class awareness represent basic types of motivation.

In films such as *Georgy Girl*, *Morgan*, and *Alfie*, people from lower social classes use sex to get to a higher social class.

Establishing and foreshadowing idiosyncrasies and traits of character. There may be a need for a scene that reveals an aspect of character the viewer needs to know in order to understand later actions by that character. If, for example, a character is going to lose his temper over an important issue at a crucial moment, it is necessary to show him losing his temper over a trivial issue earlier in the film, so the viewer will not be suddenly faced with what might be considered unacceptable behavior from the character.

Distinguishing traits of personality such as thumb sucking, fear of being touched, the need for a drink in a moment of crisis, or the desire for sexual intimacy after violence should be established if they are going to be used to move the plot forward. There is no need to establish unique traits if they will not be important within the context of the conflict.

In *The Third Man*, it was established early that the hunted man liked cats, which later was a clue used to identify him.

Names. The name of the character can make the character memorable and give a dimension. It may be helpful to use telephone books, including foreign telephone books, to find nationality names, or books on naming babies for first names. Be careful to distinguish between masculine and feminine forms of names. Ask yourself if the name fits the character.

Cultural differences

In Anglo-American films, characters tend to shout in whispers. Scenery is rarely torn; the characters rip each other emotionally, but in modified tones. Shock is often best achieved with restraint.

Who's Afraid of Virginia Woolf? is atypically uninhibited, and the viewers are as uncomfortable and embarrassed as Nick and Honey, the visitors who come upon George and Martha at war with each other.

On the other hand, film clips of Oriental or Middle Eastern funerals show mourners ripping their clothes and faces while screaming and weeping—revealing how different cultures are. Leo Rosten has described this amusingly in the preface to *A Treasury of Jewish Quotations* (McGraw-Hill):

> The English place a premium on the concealment of emotion; they voice a deep conviction as if it were a tentative opinion; they are made uncomfortable by a raised voice or a trickled tear; they disapprove of the dogmatic—and all of this puzzles people . . . who were steeped in other modalities of affect. Where Egypt wails, England blinks. Where Hindu women tear their hair, English women study their nails. An Italian explodes invective; an Englishman sniffs, "Really?" When the Russians thunder, "Everyone knows . . . ," the English demur, "But I should think that . . ." Where Americans cry, "It's terrific!" Englishmen concede, "Rather impressive." And where Englishmen murmur, "What a pity," Jews cry, "What a disaster!"

Stereotypes and cliché characters

The Bullfighter, the Artist, the Poet, the Married Woman— these are usually not people, but symbols. Group stereotypes such as gangs, New York Jews, farmboys, college boys, society girls, Irish policemen, Greek restaurateurs, or Italian thugs are clichés to be avoided. If they must be used, make them different, but not grotesque:

Not the hero who holds his liquor well,
    but one who doesn't

Not the soldier who is all courage,
    but the one who overcomes fear

Not the sweet girl next door,
    but a bitch

Not the whore with the heart of gold,
    but a venal slut

Not the frail poet,
    but one who was a football star

Not the obsequious black servant,
    but a Malcolm X

CHAPTER 5

Exposition

Primary exposition is the telling and showing to the audience the time and place of the story, the names and relationships of the characters, and the nature of the conflict. Exposition must come quickly. If a viewer doesn't know the time, the location, and the relationships between the characters, he will be lost, confused, and unable to follow the story. Minor details of exposition can be scattered throughout the action, but time, place, relationships, and locking the conflict are too basic to delay.

There is no limitation on the ways exposition can be handled. The classic method was the Greek chorus explaining the situation from two points of view. Shakespeare used a prologue read out to the audience, as in *Henry V*. Soliloquy, as in *Hamlet*, is a form of exposition. The near-subliminal projection (very short clips) used in *The Pawnbroker* exposed what the pawnbroker was thinking. The lyrics of the song "Three Coins in the Fountain" revealed the situation in the film of the same name. The inventive graphic design in the opening roll-up of *Star Wars* gave a new look to a very old expository technique.

Exposition in dialogue continues throughout the drama, shedding light on action that occurred before the story begins. This is vital to the understanding of the characters and their motivations and relationships.

Exposition of time and place

There are at least five standard techniques by which time and place are revealed:

(1) *Voice-over narrator,* as in the opening lines of *The Reivers* (screenplay by Irving Ravetch and Harriet J. Frank, Jr., © 1969):

FADE IN:

1. EXT THE TOWN - DAY

The drowsy, decorous little town of Jefferson, Mississippi, at the turn of the century, a place of simple beauty with things well built for the contentment of hardy men.

The VOICE of the NARRATOR is heard:

> NARRATOR'S VOICE
>
> When I was young, I lived in a town called Jefferson, Mississippi. That was a long time ago. Quite a few people took up the land at a dollar an acre and married one another and produced children and built houses. We were mostly farmers and mule-traders and storekeepers. There was some bragging and some lying, but on the whole, we were a pleasant and courteous people, tending to our own business. It seems to me now that those days were like an endless summer, stored with pleasure in my memory . . .

(2) *Written presentation on screen* can set not only time and place, but possibly more—"Casablanca: 1942" or "Paris: 1848"—which may or may not be double-exposed over an opening shot of the location. The opening roll-up of *Star Wars* not only describes the time and place but also provides other information needed by the viewer.

FADE IN:

1. EXT SPACE

A vast sea of stars serves as the backdrop for the MAIN TITLE.

War drums echo through the heavens, as a ROLL-UP slowly crawls into infinity ...

It is a period of civil wars in the galaxy. A brave alliance of underground freedom fighters has challenged the tyranny and oppression of the awesome GALACTIC EMPIRE.

Striking from a fortress hidden among the billion stars of the galaxy, rebel spaceships have won their first victory in a battle with the powerful Imperial starfleet. The EMPIRE fears that another defeat could bring a thousand more solar systems into the rebellion, and Imperial control over the galaxy would be lost forever.

To crush the rebellion once and for all, the EMPIRE is constructing a sinister new battle station. Powerful enough to destroy an entire planet, its completion spells certain doom for the champions of freedom.

The awesome yellow planet of Tatooine emerges from total eclipse. A tiny silver spacecraft races into view, followed by a giant Imperial starship. Hundreds of deadly laser bolts streak from the Imperial warship, causing the main solar fin of the rebel craft to disintegrate. The smoldering rebel ship is quickly overtaken by the Imperial craft.

(From the screenplay for the motion picture *Star Wars*, courtesy of Lucasfilm, © 1977 Lucasfilm Ltd.)

③ *A visual dramatization* can give important information.

In *Hud*, a new Cadillac is seen driving down a highway (the model of the car establishes the time), and passes a Texas state highway sign which establishes the location.

If a man is seen walking out of an airport and the sign above his head reads "Kennedy International Airport" or "Leonardo da Vinci: Airport Roma," we know that the story is contemporary; the place also is established. Stock shots of the New York skyline, the Eiffel Tower, or Big Ben atop Parliament quickly identify the place.

④ *Newspaper headlines, radio or television announcements,* costumes, language, signs, furniture, hairstyles, and car styles all establish time and place.

⑤ *Ballads* whose lyrics present expository information have been used effectively, as in *High Noon* and *Three Coins in the Fountain*.

Exposition of relationships

Relationships past and present between characters must be revealed if they are important to the story. That Mr. and Mrs. A are seated at dinner with Mr. and Mrs. B may be of no great interest to viewers unless it has already been revealed that Mr. or Mrs. A sleeps or has slept with Mr. or Mrs. B or vice versa. Thousands of people stand in a crowded street celebrating: What? The end of World War II? The fall of Paris? An election victory? New Year's Eve? A man and a woman are walking together: Is she his wife? Mother? Daughter? Mistress?

In addition to time, place, and relationships, exposition should reveal the nature of the world the viewer has entered, setting the mood, environment, and tone of the film.

> In the film of *The Sound of Music*, panoramic views of the Alps under the titles give a feeling of space, which is absent in the stagelike action of the story.

> Opening on the witches in *Macbeth* conveys the intellectual climate within which the film must be seen.

> Dorothy's survival of the tornado, and the first characters she meets on the road in *The Wizard of Oz*, establishes the frame of imaginative reference; so do the opening shots of *Star Wars*.

> The opening quarrel between George and Martha in *Who's Afraid of Virginia Woolf?* reveals the emotional tone of the film as well as certain basic elements of their characters.

Techniques of exposition

① A quarrel is an excellent technique for revealing information. For instance, a husband and wife quarrel:

> Wife: Ten years married to you and this damned mining town.
> Man: Go to hell. Go back to New York. Go find your Johnny.

> You'd have married him if he'd had a dime. Now he's got
> a dime.
> Wife: You're right. He's rich. He'd show me New York.

At least ten pieces of information in a very brief exchange
including revelation of character. Exposition by characters
under stress is dramatic.

(2) A simple question can beget all the required exposition:

> 1st Man: Where can I find Joe Smith?
> 2nd Man: He hasn't been here since the war, but his son runs
> the store now. His wife lives just down the street. You
> a stranger in town?
> 1st Man: Just got off the train from St. Louis.

(3) The "good companion" is less a character than an exposition technique: Hamlet's friend and confidant, Horatio; the
Lone Ranger's companion, Tonto; and Don Quixote's companion, Sancho Panza, are all good companions. They may
reveal some aspects of character, but their primary purpose
is to be spoken to.

Horatio exists so that Hamlet may have someone he can speak to
with complete honesty.

There being no camera small enough to put into the Lone Ranger's head, Tonto serves as the means of exposing the central character's thinking.

Friday serves Robinson Crusoe.

In *Track of the Cat*, Robert Mitchum was alone in his hunt for
long periods of time, and the viewer was frequently as lost in the
snow as were the characters.

(4) *Opening sequences must be more than exposition.* The conflict must be locked while the exposition is taking place in
order to hold the viewer. (See Chapter 2, *Conflict*.)

The young man driving the Cadillac in the opening of *Hud* enters
a small town, asks a man, "Have you seen my uncle Hud?" then
drives to a saloon and enters it to find the proprietor picking up
smashed furniture. The proprietor says that Hud was here and
that he is at his girlfriend's house. The Cadillac pulls up in front

of an ordinary clapboard house. The young driver honks his horn and Hud comes running out, shoes in hand, shirttail out.

All this was established within a few minutes.

⑤ *Exposition indirectly conveys the basic theme.* If a film is about illusions, about reality, about the dangers of nuclear waste, about opposition to war, about a dream gone sour, about the mystery of India—the viewer should become aware of this without being told in so many words.

If ten viewers can walk away from a film with ten different interpretations, maybe the film was about nothing specific. Perhaps they were looking at the proverbial emperor's new clothes. The marks of the artsy-craftsy film are withholding basic exposition and leaving the viewer confused. The illusion of profundity is not the same as being profound.

Of course, there may be more than one level of meaning to a specific film, but the viewer must be able to make his way from point to point. Since film is a mass medium, scripts should be written to be understood.

Other than opening exposition, other information must be treated on a need-to-know basis. Some information can be held back until the viewer needs to know it to understand what will take place next. If there is no need for the audience to know details such as family background, war record, education, or prior marriage, do not reveal them. They confuse, they delay the action, and they bury what information is needed.

If new characters are introduced in the middle of the film, or a new situation opens up, the necessary new exposition must be given to the audience.

Pitfalls to avoid in exposition

Shot directions can include information for the reader and director, but they are not part of the story. They should not say what the character is *thinking*.

①*Avoid soliloquy.* Opening with a person talking to himself rarely works.

②*Avoid the aside.* Talking to the camera is gimmicky and should be used only rarely.

③*Overheard dialogue* is passé.

④*Exposition per se,* outright explanations, slows the action. Exposition is not something to be gotten-over-with, but something to be integrated into the story.

⑤*Don't tell unnecessary details* of characters' lives or backgrounds if they are not essential for the audience to understand what happens.

⑥*Don't tell everything at once* about characters; introduce facts on a need-to-know basis.

⑦*People talk while doing.* Exposition should not bring a story to a halt. Even a party can take place with a radio telling of a victory or a divorce relevant to the story.

⑧*Flashback* is a clumsy means of exposition. It should be part of the structure. (See Chapter 3, *Structure.*)

⑨*Letters* may work on screen, but rarely on television. Don't show the letter as an insert. Better to have a voice-over of one character reading a letter aloud to another.

⑩*The telephone* is an almost static device; obviously, it worked in *Dial M for Murder,* but used for the purpose of exposition it can become a crutch.

⑪*Don't hold back on exposition,* but be subtle. If the bus pulls into a depot with a sign saying "Los Angeles to San Francisco," the viewer knows the place is San Francisco if the bus empties.

⑫ *The maid/butler opening,* in which two servants expose information while cleaning the parlor, is passé. This is equally true for any other stock characters not integral to the plot.

Final exposition is sometimes used as part of or following the denouement, with words on a screen roll telling what happened after the end of the action: "And this little boy grew up to be President." (See Chapter 3, *Structure.*)

CHAPTER 6

■

Dialogue

Function

Dialogue is one of the two most apparent parts of a screenplay. The audience is very conscious of it. The viewer looks at the screen and listens to the dialogue. The dialogue must serve four basic functions:

1. To move the storyline forward.

2. To reveal aspects of character not otherwise seen.

3. To present exposition and particulars of past events.

4. To set the tone for the film.

Dialogue must be crafted to create the illusion that this is what those characters would say within the context of this conflict. But film is a visual medium; dialogue should be kept to a minimum. If a line does not serve one of the basic functions, cut it, regardless of how clever, memorable, or poetic it is. As Willa Cather said, "Kill your darlings." The opening lines can tip the entire strength or weakness of a script. They set the tone. They are a metaphor of the entire film, as in the opening lines of *Now, Voyager:*

> WILLIAM (the butler)
> (to the maids)
> She's coming down.

> Mrs. Vale comes down the staircase.

> MRS. VALE
> We will be pouring tea in the drawing room this afternoon.

51

> WILLIAM
> (off to the maids)

Hilda!

> MRS. VALE
> Please tell Miss Charlotte to be down in ten minutes.

The basic conflict of the film is the clash between the domineering Mrs. Vale (Gladys Cooper) and her daughter, Charlotte (Bette Davis).

An ear for words

A play may survive a clumsy plot, but no play can survive a clumsy set of lines. Dialogue is not conversation; while it may create the illusion of conversation, it is selected, ordered, and purposeful. Conversation is random. What is said in a "bull session" between couples on the beach, at dinner, traveling, in an elevator, or in a crowd is conversation, not dialogue.

Seemingly naturalistic dialogue is an edited version of real talk. A scriptwriter must develop an ear for words. Not all characters talk the same way, and not all of them talk the way the writer talks. Naturalistic dialogue is an edited version of real talk.

A court transcript is organized to establish points, but it is still not dialogue. A real trial may take days, weeks, even months.

In the film *The Verdict* the entire personal story as well as the lawyer's investigation and the trial scenes ran 129 minutes in the theater and 120 minutes in a television time slot that included commercials.

Dialogue reveals character

While the best revelation of character comes from the actions performed by the character, the camera cannot fit inside his head to reveal his thoughts. Dialogue, too, reveals character. There is no other way to convey how a character thinks or why he did something springing from past action.

The best dialogue is head-to-head confrontation.

In the opening scene of *Who's Afraid of Virginia Woolf?* Martha screams at her husband George as the younger couple enter. The dialogue reveals Martha's reactions to other people and her relationship to George. In this play, which is almost all dialogue and little action, the tension, bitterness, and emotional clash conveyed by the dialogue provides the action and reveals the characters. The characters were "just talking," but they were ripping each other's guts out with what they said, assaulting each other's dreams and images of self.

Dialogue style differentiates characters.

Polonius in *Hamlet* is revealed by his wordiness.

Stanley Kowalski in *A Streetcar Named Desire* is characterized by his inability to be verbal. Blanche, his sister-in-law, is remembered for her way of talking about a mythical world.

Professor Higgins in *My Fair Lady* is known for precise and perfect English.

The characters played by Will Rogers were known for the Oklahoman's drawl.

Verbal traits reveal character.

There may be self-revelation of character through dialogue. If possible, the scriptwriter should create a speech for the protagonist and another for the antagonist in which each reveals how he sees himself and the conflict. These speeches may reveal aspects of the characters and the conflict completely different from those which the other characters and the audience know or expect. Such a speech, if viable within the context of the drama, can be used to expose the innermost feelings of a character. This is best done under stress, contemplation, or anger. The character drops his shield in an unguarded moment and reveals his self-image. For example, in the film *The Night of the Iguana*, Deborah Kerr's character reveals her past and her fantasies in one scene without interruption. Usually, however, it is safer to cut up a long speech by a question or a comment: "You really mean ... ?" "Did you say ... ?" Or repeat a word or phrase and have the speaker nod or repeat it for emphasis. (See Chapter 4, *Character*.)

Dialogue moves the plot forward

Dialogue must be spoken within the context of a conflict and move the plot forward. Ideas, dreams, visions, and love may all be discussed if the audience is kept aware of the conflict in the background. The dialogue is the vehicle for creating and resolving the conflict. A character does not talk merely to show what he is like. His utterances bear on the story as a whole, keep it moving, advancing it just as much as it needs to be advanced and at the appropriate speed.

Dialogue can serve both as a means of foreshadowing action and as a technique for transition.

> Two people sit in an office. One rises and says, "I am going to John's." The camera can then pick up a stranger, then draw back to reveal the man who was "going to John's." The audience will know the stranger is John.

Dialogue for exposition

Dialogue is necessary to explain past events and motivations that bear on the story, but this is best done after the conflict is locked. Some writers destroy a script by overloading it with preliminary exposition, as happened in Richard Brooks's *Lord Jim*. The necessity in television of grabbing the audience immediately, before the titles, has cured some writers of this mistake, but long speeches in exposition are rarely justified. (See Chapter 5, *Exposition*.)

The message need not be explained in the dialogue

> There was no need for a speech against war in *All Quiet on the Western Front*.

> There was no need for a speech against vigilante justice in *The Ox-Bow Incident*.

54

There was no need for a speech against money-making evangelism in *Elmer Gantry*.

Each film made its point without any characters declaiming on the subject. The subject of the film and the way the film is constructed should convey sufficient message. *Guess Who's Coming to Dinner* was diminished by its undramatic speeches about tolerance; no character in *Death of a Salesman* discussed the eroding quality of the American Dream gone sour. As Samuel Goldwyn is reputed to have said, "Messages are for Western Union."

Techniques and style

①*Simplicity.* Dialogue must be understandable the first time. Unlike a book, the audience cannot flip back for a re-run or pause to think about what was said. There is no time to figure out obscure language. The film goes by at twenty-four frames per second, and the audience must "get it" right away; the story moves on. Simple words, well selected and ordered, create the best dialogue. The multisyllable, elegant, or abstruse word has no place in dialogue unless it is spoken by a character to whom such a word is intrinsic to that character's role in the film.

② *Quotable lines.* Watch out for lines that seem to stand out too much. There should be no quotable lines in scripts; that is, lines that don't need the context of the specific story. Lines can be clever in the context of the film, but they should not stand out artificially. If the viewer is too aware of the language, it will distract him. Dialogue should be normal, non-intrusive language. Oratorical or highly rhetorical speech is outmoded. Understate rather than overstate.

③ *Cutting.* One of the biggest flaws in scripts is the overuse of dialogue. Too often dialogue tells the viewer what he already knows or has no need to know about the characters and the plot. Unless one is writing a film like *My Dinner with Andre* (two hours of dialogue without action), dialogue should be kept lean and should be cut wherever possible without losing clarity. Entire speeches may often be removed without damaging the structure of the scene. The simplest way to trim dialogue is inside a speech. Paddy Chayefsky, a master of dialogue, has written:

> "First cut out all the wisdom; then cut out all the adjectives. I've cut some of my favorite stuff. I have no compassion when it comes to cutting. No pity. No sympathy. Some of my dearest and most beloved bits of writing have gone out with a very quick slash, slash, slash."

④ *Dialogue and visuals too frequently duplicate.* There is no need to "show and tell" unless there is dramatic significance. Ask yourself what the question "Where is Margie?" will accomplish. If Margie is home washing her hair and the viewer already knows this, the question and the answer are not needed. If, however, the answer is "She is home washing her hair" and the viewer knows she is lying dead or in the wrong bed, the question can take on dramatic meaning.

⑤ *Dialogue should be consistent.* If a character speaks with an accent, uses bad grammar, or has a speech idiosyncrasy or handicap, he should have it throughout the film, unless there is a good dramatic reason for changing it, as in *Born Yesterday* or *My Fair Lady*.

⑥ *People speak in their own rhythm.* Good dialogue will capture the rhythm and speech patterns of each character. In *The Rose Tattoo*, the character played by Anna Magnani said:

> "Four thousand—three hundred—and eighty. The number of nights I held him all night in my arms. Sometimes I didn't sleep, just held him all night in my arms. And I am satisfied with it. I grieve for him. Yes, my pillow at night is never dry, but I am satisfied to remember."

Note the rhythm, repetition of words, specificity, flow, the concrete visual imagery.

⑦ *Dialogue is jumpy.* People think as they talk. They stumble, hesitate, and use incomplete sentences. Dialogue should be broken up by interjecting comments and reactions. Dialogue tends to bounce back and forth between the persons in a scene. If the dialogue is too obvious, a Ping-Pong game, it becomes monotonous. There should be a rhythm to phrase lengths. Repetition helps create rhythm.

> JOHN
> What do you think?

> MARY
>
> Think? Well, I think that Bill—remember Bill?

> JOHN
> Yes, I remember Bill. He was the one who . . .

> MARY
> That's right. The broken nose.

Note the repetition of words and names. *Think* three times. *Remember* twice. *Bill* three times.

⑧ *Long speeches.* Long speeches work better on the stage than on the screen. In film, there must be a very good reason for using a long speech, such as the revelation of character in the award-winning speech by Montgomery Clift in *Judgment at Nuremberg*. Few actors can handle long speeches. Hickey's monologue in *The Iceman Cometh* was superb on stage, dismal on screen.

⑨ *Visuals to enhance dialogue.* The writer must keep the picture on the screen in mind when writing dialogue. If the sequence is lengthy—two minutes or more—the writer should create a visual action for the speakers; improvisation on location is too expensive and chancey. As they speak, the characters may be in transit, undressing, washing a car, playing a computer game, walking, throwing stones in the water, etc. Break the dialogue with action and reaction. The reactions of the person being talked to must be written into the script.

(10) *Transitions and tracking.* Don't jerk the audience from place to place or from time to time. Dialogue has to indicate change of time or place. It is not necessary to show a character getting into a car, driving through traffic, stopping in front of a building, or entering the building, then the elevator, then the corridor, knocking on a door, and being allowed to enter, unless this is a backdrop for important dialogue.

Lines of dialogue track; they follow from one line to another, logically, without losing a beat. The audience must be able to follow word for word, nuance for nuance, idea for idea. One speaker may repeat words or phrases that the other speaker has used. One person may finish a sentence begun by another. Don't write one speech, then another; they must "hook." Unless there is a clear purpose for using the unrelated line or non sequitur, relate lines and link them together. There are the purposeful exceptions: A character may speak trivia to avoid a problem, and then break down or blurt out the unmentioned or unmentionable: "What are we going to do about Sarah?"

(11) *Non-verbal communication.* Eugene O'Neill said that the eloquence of our language is in its pauses, stutterings, and inability to communicate. There can be a certain elegance to silence.

In film, as opposed to stage drama, there are often long sequences without dialogue. Nods, shakes of heads, and shrugs can replace dialogue. There are times when a moan or its equivalent will be infinitely more emotional than any dialogue, such as the scene in *Mourning Becomes Electra* when Katina Paxinou starts keening at the moment of her husband's death.

(12) *Poetry.* Poetry has a place on the screen, but it is in the imagery, in the speech patterns, and in the concepts, not in the lines. The painful moment caught, the simple reaction that understates, or the rhythms of finely wrought language can be poetic.

The genius of Shakespeare makes his plays acceptable in

verse and Elizabethan vocabulary, but, in general, American audiences are actually hostile to poetry. A few plays in free verse have been filmed: Maxwell Anderson's *Winterset* and *High Tor*, Dylan Thomas's *Under Milk Wood*, and T. S. Eliot's *Murder in the Cathedral*. A number of films have been adapted from poems, but not using the original poetry in the dialogue: the jazz poem *The Set-Up* by Joseph Moncure March; *The Best Years of Our Lives*, from a poem by MacKinlay Kantor; and Longfellow's *Hiawatha*.

A character may have a poetic spirit, but he rarely expresses himself in poetry, although a particular character in a particular script may, indeed, express himself in a somewhat poetic fashion. Ours is not a time of beautiful language; speech is increasingly ordinary, but rich in slang, in breadth of vocabulary, and in vividness. A glib and verbal character may develop patterns and rhythms in his dialogue which set him apart from other characters, as the dustman father of Eliza Doolittle in *My Fair Lady*. A poetic touch can be effected by repetition of words rather than by metrical lines.

Vocabulary

The mass culture of radio and television, army service and job mobility are leveling American speech. However, not all Americans speak the same English yet. Islands of regionalism and folk idiom persist. Jargon distinguishes occupations; slang identifies time and place; the level of language identifies social status.

①*Regionalisms.* Black English, Blue Ridge English, Cajun and Creole English, etc., must be taken into account:

Does the character eat cottage cheese, smearcase, or Dutch cheese?

Drink water from a water fountain or a bubbler?

Take his shoes for repair to a cobbler or shoemaker?

Drink soda or pop?

Bait his hook with earthworms, red worms, or angle worms?

Carry a pail or a bucket?

Play on a teeter-totter or a seesaw?

Cook in a frying pan or a spider?

Regional words help to identify a character's background, and if they can be incorporated into the dialogue, they should be.

②*Jargon and slang.* A physician will use the jargon of his profession, a soldier the jargon of his. An artist or housewife will reveal by his or her vocabulary what he or she is. However, slang should be used selectively or not at all because it dates fast. A popular slang expression may be obsolete even before the film is released. Obviously, a period piece will use the vocabulary of its time, including the slang.

③*Level of language.* Speech reveals the social and intellectual background of the character, his education and circumstances. In *Pygmalion (My Fair Lady)*, George Bernard Shaw created an entire drama about social differences reflected in levels of speech. When writing dialogue, the question must always be asked, "Is this what this character would say and is this the way he would say it?" A college graduate does not speak like a thug. A thug is unlikely to speak like a college graduate. A lawyer is rarely nonverbal. *Dese, dem,* and *dose* are not used, but bad grammar is, at some educational levels. All characters are not equally intelligent or equally educated, and their speech reflects this.

Circumstances will alter a character's vocabulary. A soldier in a barracks will speak differently than he will at a briefing with a general officer present. The informal speech used at home or at play by a scholar is not the level of speech used by the same scholar addressing an academic conference. Sentence structure is different for different ethnic groups. An Irish American might say, "It's sorry I am," or "I'm after buying a new car."

④*Accents.* Dialogue should be written without attempting to capture accents or national intonations by misspelling. If

60

the character speaks with a French, German, or Cockney accent, this should be stated in the slug line describing the character when he is first introduced.

If the writer wants a Southern or Western drawl, he should say that is the way the character speaks. Trying to show this by misspelling can only mislead. Authenticity can best be captured by the use of regionalisms or period language, by sentence structure, and by word order.

If the character uses a foreign word or expression, this should be in the dialogue so long as the viewer understands it in its context. The nature and extent of dialect will be determined by the actor with the director.

⑤ *References.* In addition to a standard American dictionary and thesaurus, the serious scriptwriter will find specialized dictionaries valuable. To name a few:

> *Dictionary of American Regional English,* Volume I, A-C, Frederic G. Cassidy, Chief Editor; Harvard University Press, 1985. (Only the first volume of a projected five has been published.)

> *Dictionary of Foreign Terms in the English Language,* David Carroll; Hawthorn Books, 1973.

> *Western Words: A Dictionary of the American West,* Ramon F. Adams; University of Oklahoma Press, 1968.

> *The Underground Dictionary,* Eugene E. Landy; Simon & Schuster, 1971.

> *Dictionary of American Slang,* Harold Wentworth and Stuart Berg Flexner; Thomas Y. Crowell, 1967.

> *A Dictionary of Americanisms,* Mitford M. Mathews; University of Chicago Press, 1951.

> *Brewer's Dictionary of Phrase & Fable,* revised by Ivor H. Evans; Harper & Row, 1970.

A few minutes spent with the library's card catalogue will provide specialized dictionaries of Afro-American slang, Air Force, soldier, and sailor slang, erotic and scatological terms, cowboy slang, underworld slang, a gay lexicon, hash-house lingo, Cockney, and many more. Note dates of usage to avoid the use of anachronisms.

Emotion expressed through dialogue

Understatement in emotional reaction is the norm in American drama. Americans, Englishmen, and West Europeans tend to shout in whispers. This can result in a lack of flamboyance, theatricality, spectacle, fervor, gusto, and visceralism. It can also produce bland, dull films. On the other hand, emotional overstatement leads easily to the cheapest melodrama. Good screenwriting must achieve balance, using understatement and theatricality each in its own place.

It is better to embarrass than to bore. Uninhibited emotional scenes can embarrass the viewers. *The Iceman Cometh*, *Who's Afraid of Virginia Woolf?*, and *The Glass Menagerie* were in large part successful because they did embarrass the viewers by their intimacy and made them feel like Peeping Toms. Great screenwriting does not avoid audience embarrassment based on real emotion.

Pitfalls to avoid in writing dialogue

①*Overusing first names.* Strangers who have been introduced do not continue to use names when speaking unless the situation is formal, such as a job interview or a legal situation. The first time the characters appear, names can be used to establish the characters for the viewers. If there are three or more persons present during a discussion and the speaker wishes to single one out, he may very well address him by name. Otherwise, this will be considered an affectation on the part of the character. It may be an idiosyncrasy used to create the personality of the character if it adds a dimension that will help to understand him better.

John: What do you think, Bill?
Bill: Well, John, I think that we should . . .

This is clumsy. It is obvious that the two know each other. Two people who know each other will eat together or sleep together without resorting to names.

②*Long speeches can be deadly on screen.* One passage of dialogue running more than five or six lines should be studied with great care for trimming, cutting, or breaking up. Few actors, actresses, writers, or directors have the extraordinary skill to carry a long speech. Don't take star quality into account in your writing. The superstar you want or expect to be reciting your lines may not be interested or available.

③*Avoid soliloquy.* People do not talk to themselves on screen. This is an easy out for the amateur. Find another way to get that piece of information across.

④*Don't use asides.* Passé.

⑤*Don't use a narrator* in a dramatic script unless it is a documentary effect that is wanted, as in *The House on 92nd Street* or *To the Ends of the Earth*, where it is used to make the story appear authentic.

⑥*Avoid non sequiturs.* Each person's dialogue should flow from previous lines.

⑦*The words* yes *and* no *are rarely necessary.* Characters nod or shake their heads. Omit unnecessary dialogue if a visual reaction is possible.

⑧*Don't have one character swear at another.* It doesn't work. Express the anger in normal dialogue, or have the actor reveal anger without using words—shake his fist, clench his hands, frown, etc.

⑨*Formal introductions are clumsy and time consuming.* When a character is first seen, it may be advisable to use his name so that if he is referred to later, the viewer will know who he is.

(10) *Remember the budget when writing lines for extras.* If one word is spoken by an "extra," he must be paid the minimum rate for a full day.

(11) *Don't write your autobiography.* What will you do for an encore?

(12) *Avoid coincidence in dialogue as well as action.* Two people saying the same thing may seem to be amusing, but it is rarely worth the effort and should be avoided unless it is important to the plot.

(13) *Avoid trite transitions.* Don't have a character say "I'm not going to . . ." and then cut to a scene in which he is doing just what he said he wouldn't do. There are many variations of this cliché.

(14) *Avoid verbal clichés such as:*

"It's quiet . . . too quiet."

"They're playing our song!"

"You look like you've seen a ghost!"

"Don't look back . . . I want to remember you like this."

"Hold me closer, darling, don't ever let me go!"

"There's only one doctor can save him."

"I've been blind—*blind,* I tell you!"

"He had a fighting heart."

"Pull yourself together!"

If you are going to use a cliché on purpose, point it out:

"This may be a cliché, but . . ."

"I know you may have heard this before, but . . ."

"I wish there were a better way to say 'I love you,' but . . ."

"Follow that car," and the cabbie responds, "I've always wanted to do that!"

⑮ *Avoid ending a scene with witty dialogue.* The clever re-mark, or one heavy with significance, detracts from the emo-tional impact and slows the dramatic action.

⑯ *Don't write in too much dialogue direction.* The actor and director can work out whether the line calls for a frown, a smile, a shrug, or a sneer.

Make sure the last line of dialogue in the film is strong

Give the audience something to leave the theater with; they will remember the final moment and final words.

Part 2

CHAPTER 7

The Look of a Professional Script

A script is a blueprint for making a film. A successful University of Southern California Cinema Department graduate, John Milius (screenwriter of *Apocalypse Now*), advises today's students, "A script is half-sold or half-unsold, depending on the look." Typing errors, bad spelling, incorrect grammar, or the wrong form make a bad first impression, and there may be no chance to make a second impression. Michael Ludmer, as a story editor at Universal Studios, said, "I just can't bring myself to read the overdirected script." The point that each of them was making was that one of the signs of a professional screenwriter is that his script looks like a script.

There has been a kind of nonsense expressed in recent years that says that film scripts are a literary form. They may accidentally become that, but no one who works in film cares about that. Agent, producer, story editor, director, actor—all want a literate script that looks like a script and tells them what is going to take place on the screen. If the script is in proper form, a production manager can figure out what it will cost to make. And more important, the script will be read with understanding and respect.

Sometimes would-be scriptwriters forget that a script is for shooting. Most beginners have not seen an actual shooting script. There are scripts in print, but these are usually publisher's versions. To save money, publishers often reduce the number of pages that the shooting script would require in print, drop the shots and the information slug line, and set the speaking character's name on the left-hand margin, the way they set up a stage play. This technique does save space, but it does not produce a shooting script; it reduces the script to the information that might interest a historian or a critic, but not a filmmaker.

The standard length for a theatrical film is 100 minutes; that is about 120 pages of script. It is better if the script comes in at 125 to 130 pages than 100 to 110 pages; it is more difficult to lengthen material than to cut it.

The standard shooting script form is a simple thing to learn. Too many beginning writers worry too much about *how* to make the deal to get their story on the screen and not enough about *what* is going on the screen.

The parts of a script are few. The first thing one usually sees at the beginning of a script is FADE in:. That always goes on the left-hand margin. Some scripts end with FADE OUT: and that should go on the right-hand margin, but most writers do not bother with it.

The next item in a script is called the slug line or information line. It should always be in caps and always carry the same basic information in the same order:

INT *(interior)* or EXT. *(exterior)*
SHOT *(types)*
LOCATION
SUBJECT
NIGHT

Obviously, if the scene is taking place outside, the INT becomes EXT. There is no need to repeat INT or EXT unless you change the location, though some good scriptwriters will change or repeat this information if they come to the end of what they consider a scene—not a shot—and begin a new one.

The kinds of shots seem to confuse readers as well as writers, and over the years they have had different meanings. Many scripts will leave this piece of the slug line out and leave the decision to the director and cameraman. But if the writer decides to call the shots because they are important to the action, there are very few to keep in mind:

(*1*) CLOSE SHOT: The camera is tight on the subject. A CLOSE SHOT of John's face is just that; a CLOSE SHOT of his hands is just that.

Abbreviations CS or CU (from the older *close-up*) are almost never used anymore. There is one other affectation that one sees less and less in a script, the TIGHT CLOSE SHOT or TIGHT CLOSE-UP (TCU), but it is not needed. If the shot must focus on face, eyes, or hands, all that is needed is CLOSE SHOT FACE or CLOSE SHOT EYES, etc.

(2) MEDIUM SHOT (not MS or MED SHOT; old hands write it out): This designation covers a multitude of possibilities: one or more persons, if they are tightly grouped about a table; one person if all we want of him is his head and shoulders or his body from the waist up; or even what takes place in one room. Calling TWO SHOTS and THREE SHOTS can become foolish, such as SIX SHOT. If there are six people in a shot, one would not handle it that way. JOHN MARY GROUP is description enough.

(3) FULL SHOT (a large object fills the frame): FULL SHOT ROOM, or FULL SHOT BED, or FULL SHOT CAR are self-explanatory. This is used in some cases as an ESTABLISHING SHOT, which can reveal a city or a house in its setting. It must be followed by a shot that brings the camera in closer, because its basic purpose is just what it says—establishing relationships of people and objects or just buildings and grounds.

(4) LONG SHOT (the subject is small in the frame because of distance): The man two blocks away, the car speeding a quarter of a mile away on the road, or the horse coming across a plain is generally established as a LONG SHOT.

There are a few other shots used infrequently. The AERIAL SHOT or COPTER SHOT is just what it says it is. The INSERT SHOT is what it says it is. A man opens a drawer and looks into it. Then the writer can call an *insert shot* of what he wants the audience to see in the drawer. Or someone takes out a letter and stares at it, and if the writer wants the audience to see that, he writes INSERT SHOT LETTER. The nice thing about insert shots is that the cast, sound men, and most of the crew do not have to be wasting time on the set when these are taken at the end of the day.

The writer must be familiar with the different shots even though the director may not use the shots the writer has called. Some years ago Jerry Lewis lectured in the USC Cin-

71

ema Department, and a student asked him if directors want the writers calling shots. He answered, "I do. Always." Later in the lecture, he was asked, "Mr. Lewis, do you pay any attention to the shots the writer puts down?" And he answered, "Never. Who is he to tell me where to put my camera?"

Locations are important in the slug line. They follow the **SHOT**, if given: **FARM, BEDROOM, KITCHEN, BUSY URBAN STREET**, whatever is needed to leave no doubt as to where the scene is to take place.

The next item on that slug line is the *subject:* **JOHN, JOHN MARY, JOHN MARY BILL CROWD**, anyone who is in the shot when the camera starts to roll. Identify a character in the slug line the first time he appears in the script, even if the audience does not know his name at that point. Describe him and give his name even if it is not spoken in the first scene in which he appears.

The last part of the slug line is **NIGHT** or **DAY**. Like **INT** or **EXT**, **NIGHT** or **DAY** need not be repeated unless there is a change. If the entire film takes place at night, then the word need appear only once, at the end of the first slug line; if it changes, the slug line must indicate the change. Some writers will go for **DUSK** or **DAWN**, and this is not wrong, although the writer should remember the problems of getting a crew or cast out at strange hours and the extra cost of doing so.

And so the slug line **INT MEDIUM SHOT BEDROOM MARY NIGHT** tells exactly what the crew needs to know. The production manager can plan the shot, the cast knows who will be in it, and the lighting men set up accordingly.

There are a few variations in the slug line, but these are simple. When the writer wants the camera to shoot out of a window and show a car driving up a driveway, the slug line should read **INT/EXT DRIVEWAY CAR DAY**. If he wants the camera to peep into a window, he uses **EXT/INT**, and any director will know what he has in mind.

One camera direction that confuses beginners and even some professionals is the **POV**. This means point of view. In such a shot the camera is serving as someone's eyes.

INT/EXT MEDIUM SHOT CAR JOHN'S POV DAY

Anyone reading it will know that John is looking at the car. However, that shot had better have one before it showing John looking out of the window, or the audience will not know it is John who is looking at the car. No one can be seen in his own POV unless he is passing a window or mirror, because he cannot see himself, at least not his own face. (A student script called for this shot: JOHN SITTING THISTLE'S POV.)

The next line of a script is the shot description. It is single-spaced, follows the full margins of the script, is double-spaced below the slug line, and is generally written in present-tense prose. This line is very important: It is where the writer describes the action.

```
INT MEDIUM SHOT BEDROOM MARY NIGHT

Mary, about twenty-three, slim, casually dressed in
jeans, stands for a moment looking toward the window.
PAN with her as she walks across the room and settles
down on the bed. JOHN ENTERS and SLAMS the door
behind him. JOHN is thirty, executive type, and
ruggedly handsome. Mary looks up at him. Both smile.
```

Here we have a description of the two characters that will help a casting director know the types he is looking for; the action is described. Caps are used to indicate the camera movement *within* a shot, and John's entrance is in caps because he was not in the shot when the camera started rolling. The sound man and later the sound editor should be aware that the door slams. All sound effects are pointed out by describing them in caps: GUN FIRES. CAR BACKFIRES.

A shot description is just that: a description of the action that the writer wants shot. Nothing else that takes place in this scene in this room need have a slug line again; it is a Master Scene.

This leaves only two more items in the look of the script: the dialogue and dialogue direction. The name of the person speaking is double-spaced below the shot description, is always centered on the page, and has the same margin for each speaker; when necessary, it is followed by dialogue direction, which is single-spaced. The actual dialogue, also single-spaced, then follows:

                    JOHN
              (dialogue direction)
         What the hell did you think you were doing,
         walking out on Bill like that?

                    MARY
         I don't give a damn what he thinks.

John walks over to stand looking down at her.

                    MARY (cont'd)
                  (furious)
         You going to hit me or something?

The margins line up for the dialogue directions. The fact that a character continues speaking after a direction is indicated beside the name.

There are two means of indicating the dialogue when the character is not on the screen:

JOHN (VO) means that John is narrating voice-over and is not on the screen. He may be telling what he is thinking or something about his childhood with an appropriate visual on screen. He is the narrator. If the narrator has no name, then he is simply indicated as NARRATOR (VO).

However, when John is in the scene, but he is not in the shot, then use JOHN (OS), and the reader, the editor, and the director know that John is present but off screen. The camera is not on him when this shot is taken, but John's voice is to be heard while the camera is on someone or something else.

Don't let your margins slop over. The dialogue should *never* get confused with the stage directions. The dialogue direction margins should never run as wide as the dialogue margins. The dialogue margins must be sufficiently narrow so that they do not become confused with the stage directions at the right or left margin. If there is a DISSOLVE TO: that goes on the *right-hand margin*, double-spaced below the last part of the shot. It is a form of visual punctuation to indicate that

74

time has passed. It is used less and less often. There is no
need to call CUT TO: because if it is not a FADE OUT or a
DISSOLVE TO: it is taken for granted it is going to be a CUT
TO:. There is little left that it could be.

The professional look of a script is not difficult to achieve.
(See the sample from the shooting script of *Back to the Future.*) There may be minor variations in the typing instructions from one studio to another, but the basic script form
described here is the way a story editor, an agent, a producer,
a director, a production manager, or an actor would expect
it to look. These are the people who, along with the rest of
the crew, will have to work with it as a blueprint. It does not
limit the writer's right to indicate what he wants the film to
look like. Instead, it helps people to meet his desire, and it
can be used as a working tool.

Rev. 2/28/85

''BACK TO THE FUTURE''   Pg. 1*

A1 INT BROWN'S GARAGE (1985) — DAY   A1

CLOSE ON A TICKING CLOCK, showing 2 minutes to 8.

CAMERA MOVES, exploring, revealing MORE CLOCKS, of all
varieties—cuckoo clocks, digital clocks, a grandfather
clock, Felix the Cat with moving eyes . . . and all of
them are ticking away in DEAD SYNC.

We continue exploring the garage, noting (in no
particular order) a jet engine, a stack of unpaid bills
addressed to ''Dr. E. Brown'' marked ''OVERDUE,''
automotive tools, electronics parts, discarded Burger
King wrappers, a video camera, an unmade army cot.

We go past a CLOCK RADIO——it lights up and comes on.

                    RADIO ANNOUNCER (VO)
          . . . weather for Hill Valley and vicinity for
          today, Friday, October 25: partly cloudy with a
          chance of drizzles . . .

Now we come to a COFFEE MAKER with a built-in clock
timer. It too turns on——only there is no coffee pot!
Boiling coffee drips onto an already wet hot plate.

Another timer triggers a TV set——an A.M. NEWSCAST is
in progress, and the ANCHORWOMAN talks against a slide:
''Plutonium Theft?'' with the yellow and purple
radiation symbol.

                    ANCHORWOMAN (ON TV)
          . . . Officials at the Pacific Nuclear Research
          Facility have denied the rumor that a case of
          missing plutonium was in fact stolen from their
          storehouse two weeks ago. A Libyan terrorist
          group had claimed responsibility for the alleged
          theft. Officials now attribute the discrepancy to
          a simple clerical error. The FBI, which is still
          investigating the matter, had no comment . . .

We pass a TOASTER attached to a timer. Two pieces of
black toast sit on it, and as the timer clicks on, the
ashen toast drops into the toaster . . . again.
Clearly, we are seeing a morning routine for someone
who hasn't been home for a while.

                                          Rev. 11/7/84

                                          Pg. 22-B.*

17 EXT TWIN PINES MALL PARKING LOT - NIGHT   17

CAMERA PANS from the lit entrance sign, depicting 2
PINE TREES IN A ROW with ''TWIN PINES MALL'' in
lettering below (along with a digital clock at 1:18) to

pick up MARTY on his skateboard with WALKMAN AND VIDEO CAMERA. Marty skateboards around a corner of the mall and sees

AN OVERSIZED STEP-VAN with a drop down tailgate (like a ramp) all by itself on the vast, sodium-vapor-lit parking lot. It's beat up and has lettered on the side, ''DR. E. BROWN ENTERPRISES – 24 HOUR SCIENTIFIC SERVICE.''

A large DOG sits patiently beside it. The animal has a battery operated digital clock attached to its collar. There are a few boxes, some equipment, and a suitcase nearby.

MARTY skateboards over to the truck and the dog.

> MARTY
> Doc? Hello?
> (to the dog, petting him)
> Hiya, Einstein. Where's the Doc? Where's the Doc, boy?

We hear an ENGINE REV UP–––the truck engine?

The rear truck doors suddenly open and a SLEEK STAINLESS STEEL DELOREAN drives down the drop down gate, onto the parking lot. It's been modified with coils and some wicked looking units on the rear engine.

Marty stares at it in amazement.

The DeLorean pulls up to him and stops. The gull wing driver's door opens and out steps DR. EMMETT BROWN, 65.

He's clad in a white radiation suit, hood off. His hair
is wild, his eyes are full of life and energy.

          BROWN
    Good evening, Marty. Welcome to my latest
    experiment. This is the big one----the one I've
    been waiting for all my life.

Marty ogles the vehicle.

          MARTY
    It's a DeLorean----but what did you do to it? And
    what's with the Devo suit?

                       CONTINUED

Note: A script is always typed on paper measuring 8½ x 11
inches. The excerpt from the script for *Back to the Future* has
been reduced to fit this book's dimensions.

CHAPTER 8

━━━━

Production Considerations

Camera

The scriptwriter should not indicate camera angles unless necessary, as in a required shot from a roof of a building to the street. Otherwise the writer describes the *action*, not the shots, and leaves the camera angles to the director and cameraman. If the script is poor, fancy camera angles can't save it.

Don't break up the master scene. Don't write in "2-shot," "3-shot," or "another angle." Let the director break up the master scene. As a character moves from one place to another, the writer must call each shot; one for each set-up in a new location.

Camera and dialogue. Never break down shots for dialogue or "Ping-Pong" shots of close-ups. Just indicate a medium shot of three people and write the dialogue. Don't call each close-up as each person talks.

Movement is expensive. Dolly tracks are expensive. Do not waste time and money on panning entrances and exits unless relevant to the plot.

Process shots can be effective, but the writer must know that it can be done: The character described as running out of a place in flames may not be able to burn (safely) as described. Process shots must include a description of the background, which must also be filmed: "Paris" or "steps of

79

church" or "car driving down street," etc. If the writer knows that stock footage exists, it can be written into the script to be intercut in the editing. Stock footage on such scenes as a nuclear blast, for instance, can save a lot of money. If only one shot calls for a character to walk down a London street, it can be done as a rear screen projection rather than taking a whole crew to London.

Do not write JOHN ENTER LEFT or MARY WALKS DOWN THE STREET RIGHT. The set has not been built and no one knows where or how it is going to be set up for shooting. Though a writer should think visually, there are some limitations as to what can be designated physically in advance, and "lefts" and "rights" are high among those limitations.

Montage. Specifics must be written into the script so the director knows what to shoot. A montage sequence is expensive to shoot and too often is used needlessly. A montage to create the image of an earthquake (as in *San Francisco*), a great fire (as in *Elmer Gantry*), or a war (as in *War and Peace*) has a specific purpose in the plot. Planning three days of camera work on the burning of the tabernacle in *Elmer Gantry*, director Richard Brooks found himself spending three weeks with cast and crew. As this was the climax of the film and a necessity in telling the story, the cost was believed to be justified.

The montage designed to show two people falling in love over a period of time in many locations may be valid, but costume changes and location changes may be too expensive to justify the montage. Quick cuts of action in one place, as in *The Champion*, can give the effect of montage.

The "revelation pan" (people talking about someone or something followed by the camera drawing back to reveal a surprise) has its uses but is often overused.

Cinema verité. Sheer reproduction is total realism; total realism is not the stuff of drama. Cinema verité carried to its ultimate would allow for a camera to be placed for hours at a street corner to record what passes. The unedited film that has not been ordered and selected—structured—would be unbearably dull.

Nevertheless, the handheld or subjective camera can be an effective technique, as in the accidental fire scene aboard the B-52 in *Dr. Strangelove.*

Care must be used in the subjective POV, in which the camera is the eye of the protagonist, as in *Lady in the Lake.* It is necessary to first establish who is doing the watching— whose eye the camera is pretending to be. Used properly, as in the hunt scene in *Tom Jones,* shot from horseback, or the scene of the knockout and carrying the boxer back to the locker room in *Requiem for a Heavyweight,* it is effective.

The "match dissolve" is gimmicky and should be used sparingly. There should be a good reason for dissolving from a car wheel to a roulette wheel, from hands holding to the same girl holding someone else's hands. The first and second wheel do not mean much, but the match dissolve on the hands tells a lot.

"Dissolve to . . ." or "cut to . . ." are unnecessary in the script. Just write the next scene.

Avoid visual clichés.

One cigarette in the ashtray—next shot, full ashtray.

First drink, then next shot the empty bottle.

Weather changes: shot of spring, summer, fall, winter.

Pages falling from a calendar.

If a time transition is needed, invent something new.

Children and animals

These create major production problems in a script. State laws limit the number of hours and conditions under which children can work. Animals can be difficult and expensive to film; the ASPCA representative must be part of the budget. For long periods of time, *Dr. Doolittle* was able to be filmed only a single shot a day. Obviously, if a good story depends upon their presence, children and animals belong in the script.

Weather

Practically speaking, it is hard to invent weather; rain and snow are expensive to produce, require extra costumes, and should not be described unless they are integral to the story. Dawn and dusk shots mean extra money for overtime crews.

Shot descriptions for large action

It is impossible and unnecessary for the writer to describe the detailed action of a fight, but he can tell the fight's general direction and end. There is a famous line in the script of the Warner Brothers' film *The Charge of the Light Brigade* that reads simply, "They charge." The details of the action were left to the director. The same thing probably happened with the direction of the chariot race in *Ben Hur*. However, the writer should call the action and the exterior shots of an auto race, a horse chase, a mob scene, or war action as *stage directions*. (See Chapter 7, *The Look of a Professional Script*.)

Numbering shots

The writer should *not* number his shots. That may seem strange, because anyone who has seen a shooting script has seen the numbers in the margin. The shots are numbered only when the script is approved and ready for mimeograph, before cross-plotting by the production and budget managers. Otherwise, the script will have to account for every single scene number. If there is a cut in the script, it will have to read SHOT 302 to 310 OMITTED, or, if inserted, shots will have to read 302A, 302B, etc. (The theatrical script historically numbered the shots in the left-hand margin. The television director, working in a hurry and not wanting to bother opening his entire notebook, writes the numbers in the right-hand margin. If the script is for theatrical film, the left-hand margin remains standard.)

Music

Do not call the music or describe it in a script unless particular instruments or a radio or television set are to be seen on screen playing specific music that is relevant to the plot. The producer and the music director earn their salaries and resent anyone else trying to do their jobs. Even if a writer feels strongly that he wants a particular musical number, no one else may. Or it might not be available. The producer may prefer to deal with a composer and to create music from which they can both earn royalties.

CHAPTER 9

———

Other Forms and Techniques

Synopsis

In addition to the possibility of employment as a story analyst, writers should know how to prepare a synopsis and a treatment of their own scripts to show agents and prospective buyers, who may not take the time to read the whole script. Writing a synopsis (one to three pages) and a treatment (thirty to fifty pages) also helps the writer clarify his own view of the script: If he cannot reduce his story to a two-page synopsis, he doesn't know what the story is about. If he cannot describe it in a coherent, present-tense, narrative treatment, he may not *have* a story. There is a danger that a story told in thirty pages will not yield a 100- to 125-page script for a 100-minute feature film; this, too, the writer can learn early and perhaps remedy. Again it is easier to cut a too-long script than to extend a short one. (See Chapter 3, *Structure*.)

Form. Most studios have their own topsheet format for synopses (see sample, pages 85–88). The topsheet is a time-saving device for studio executives. They can see the title, author, form (screenplay, 140 pp. or novel, Bantam Publishers), type (Western, comedy, etc.), time (period setting? modern?), reader's name, and whether or not it is recommended. The body of the synopsis will be single-spaced, in the present tense, and the description of the theme should come first; it can be as short as one line, but never longer than one paragraph. The description of the theme should contain only the essence of the story: "The rise and fall of a professional prostitute." If the theme does not interest the producer, he need not read further.

The first time a character is mentioned, whether from a novel or screenplay, the name is in CAPS and he/she is identified. When the same character is mentioned later, he should be clearly identified; the person reading the synsopsis should not have to refer back to the original introduction of the character.

In synopsizing a novel, the reader must select which elements to keep and which to ignore if the story is to be filmed. Depending on the story editor's directives, the story analyst may or may not restructure a story to make it understandable. For example, the novel *From Here to Eternity* was 833 pages. It was synopsized in thirty-three pages. In the novel there were simultaneous stories of many different characters. In the synopsis, the key characters were selected and their roles in the story told. The movie was made and structured from the synopsis, not from the novel.

Reader's comments. At the end of a synopsis the reader comments on whether or not and *why* the script or novel is picture material; e.g., "fresh approach to a Western, "spine-tingling mystery," "evokes powerful emotions," or "unusual, authentic ethnic flavor," etc. The reader may say here that he likes the characters but not the plot, or the plot but not the dialogue, or why it is not recommended.

Sample Topsheet and Synopsis

OBELISK, Inc.

To: Jack Warner, Jr.
Title: TAOS

Author: Irwin R. Blacker
Category: Historical saga

Circa: 1600s
Location: Territory of New Mexico
Format: Novel, 478 pp.
Read by: Susan Craig

Theme: The peaceful Pueblo Indians are led into a deadly revolt against their Spanish oppressors.

It is 1680 in Nuevo Mexico when the chief medicine man of the Pueblos, POPÉ, has a vision that he has been ordered by the gods to rid the land of its Spanish oppressors. Popé adheres steadfastly to the belief that only when the last Spaniard is dead will his people be free. Motivated by a fierce hatred, Popé ties a rope in nine knots, one to be untied each dawn by a runner who will alert the enslaved Indians that the time has come for a revolt. On the ninth dawn, the Pueblos will rise as one to throw off the cursed Spanish. Although Popé has grave misgivings as his plan goes into action, he is unable to back down . . . and the revolt is under way. . . .

DON ANTONIO DE OTERMIN, Governor of the Spanish Province of Nuevo Mexico, faces a nearly hopeless situation as he intercepts the message of the knotted ropes and realizes that an Indian uprising is in the making. Deeply disappointed by his Nuevo Mexico post, which he believes to be a god–forsaken, desolate territory, Don Antonio nevertheless must rally his small garrison and attempt to protect the Christians, Spanish, and Indian alike.

In a surprise move, Popé appoints JUAN as his War Chief. Juan is an Indian who has divided loyalties because he respects his boss, DON JAIME MARCOS, who governs Taos, and he has fallen in love with Don Jaime's daughter, MANUELA. Juan must use the fighting skills he has learned from Don Jaime against him and his own people. After a resounding defeat of Don Antonio's forces at Sante Fe, Juan must lead his army to Taos. Juan is deeply ashamed of the task he must accomplish to remain loyal to his Indian background.

Before Juan can attack Don Jaime's hacienda, Don Jaime blows up his place, killing himself. The pueblo of Taos is effectively destroyed as Indian leader ASKON outnumbers Don Antonio. Luckily, Don Jaime's daughter,

Manuela, is safely exiled to the desert. Juan joins
Askon and shares his expert skill as a commander. Don
Antonio is injured by Askon and devastated by the
losses he sustains. This grief drives Don Antonio to
take his housekeeper, MARIA, as his lover in hope that
he can ease his own pain and impending defeat.

An Indian celebration led by Popé burns Spanish books
and art treasures. As the Spaniards flee, Juan wonders
if Popé's rule will be just as tyrannical as Don
Antonio de Otermin's. Popé's first act as victor is to
denounce Juan in an attempt to retain all the power.
Juan accepts his banishment which he uses to find
Manuela. He chooses to live a life with her in the
wilds of Nuevo Mexico.

Embittered Popé cannot understand why he is unable to
derive any satisfaction from the successful revolt. The
Spaniards have been forced from the territory, their
churches have been burned, their books destroyed: Why
isn't he happy? Popé decides that he has not
accomplished the most important thing of all, he has
not killed the white man's god.

Don Antonio de Otermin leads his refugees to the
safety of the Mexican border. He appoints weak, corrupt
FRAY JULIO as the head priest—a miraculous conversion
that stirs his people. One of the people, LUIS
QUINTANA, who harbors a grudge that he was not
appointed second in command, rallies opposition against
Don Antonio and successfully accuses him of negligence
and misconduct. Don Antonio is crushed that he has
simply been used. In seeing this truth and accepting
the fact he cannot return to Spain, he finds a new
freedom. Freely, he admits his love to Maria and vows
that he will fight the charges against him. He will
marshal his forces, form a new army, and reconquer
Nuevo Mexico. Then he will embrace Maria and they will
live happily. . . .

******

COMMENT:

Here is a masterful piece that has it all. The action
is fierce, the characters are larger than life, the
attention to divided loyalties is superb, the sweeping
historical setting is compelling, and most of all the
characters change in ways that are meaningful and
accessible. I suggest the scope, detail, and character
alliances of this material would be best represented by
a miniseries.

Juan is a pivotal force between the two opposing
factions of the Pueblo Indians and the Spaniards.
Neither Popé nor Don Antonio ever lets go of his need
to control long enough to establish a lasting peace. A
miniseries developed from this material will benefit
from showing Juan as the clear intersection of these
warring forces and as the hope for a peaceable future.
Juan's relationship with Manuela is a strong and tender
love story that stands in clear contrast to Don
Antonio's quiet desperation for a companion in Maria.
The dialogue is superb. The structure is rock solid.
And most of all the characters and their struggle can
carry interest from night to night.

RECOMMENDED.

Full treatments. If a producer becomes interested in a
property after reading a synopsis, he may want to read a
treatment that gives him a full description of the whole story
in thirty to fifty pages in present-tense, narrative form. He
may ask the studio story analyst to write the treatment, but,
if he asks the screenwriter to prepare the treatment, this service must be negotiated and paid for. (See Chapter 10, *The
Business of Filmmaking.*)

Some established writers will write a "selling script" that
contains more detailed descriptions than a "shooting script,"
but it is better for a beginner to write a full treatment for his
agent's use.

Adaptations

The adapter's obligation to the original work. The adapter (or his employer, producer, or studio) must have paid for the rights to the original property before one word of the adaptation is written. The adapter owes nothing to the original but the spirit, the theme, and the premise.

A film has different requirements and possibilities than a novel, a short story, or a play. A play, which is fairly static on stage, can be opened up and taken to many different locations. Characters as well as episodes can be added or deleted. The order of events can be changed. One rarely uses a novelist's original dialogue, even if that novelist is Hemingway: Lines that sound fine on a page of a novel often seem dull and flat when played on screen.

Dangers inherent in slavish transposition from novel to screenplay. Often the adapter ruins a film by trying to be too faithful to the original. For example, Richard Brooks's adaptation of Joseph Conrad's *Lord Jim* did not start in the right place. Almost an hour was spent in setting up the background and character of Jim before he stepped aboard the ship from which he later jumped. Dramatically, it is only with Jim's leaving the ship that the story really begins. That act creates the problem that follows Jim to the end of the film and is resolved in his death. Originally, Brooks had planned to leave the novel's narrator out of the film, but critics of his earlier film *Elmer Gantry* had been very harsh in their criticism of the changes he had made. Consequently, in adapting *Lord Jim*, Brooks remained too faithful to the original at the expense of the film. In contrast, Paul Osborne's adaptation of John Steinbeck's *East of Eden* started on page 460 of the novel and was a smashing success.

On the other hand, there is such respect for the plays of William Shakespeare that no screenwriter would dare to rewrite his lines. Adaptation is left to the ingenuity of the director in interpreting the play.

There are books written specifically to be films, as was the case with *Of Mice and Men* (novel by John Steinbeck, screenplay by Eugene Solow), *The Misfits* (Arthur Miller), *The Maltese Falcon* (screenplay by John Huston). More and more modern novelists are writing with an eye to film sales; conversely, producers often ask for a novelization of a screenplay on the assumption that a book, particularly a bestseller, creates an automatic audience for the film and gives the film added stature.

Some important differences between a film and a novel:

The scriptwriter must show the character physically and in costume; the novelist leaves more to the imagination. Not surprisingly, the script may violate the reader's image of the characters in the novel.

In a novel, if the hero and heroine are separated, it works; this rarely works in film.

What is described in a book narratively must be made visual and put into dialogue in the film.

In a novel, major reactions or decisions can be taken by an unaccompanied character. In film, there must be another person in the scene for him to talk to.

Expositional techniques are different: Time can be covered by a sentence in a novel; it must be exposed in a movie.

In a film, every action or word ought to count; in a novel, digressions are common. The film must focus on one moment of time and develop it while skipping a thousand other moments in the same story.

A novelist can write in thousands of persons or miles with a few words; the scriptwriter must show these or omit them.

The basic difference between the film script and all other forms is dramatic structure. A successful adapter must find the climax, the crises, the proper place to open and close, and the visual aspects. If the story is not the reason the property was bought (perhaps a famous author's name or a bestseller), the adapter is in trouble. He will try to save the idea, the characters, and the storyline, but in working out a dramatic story he may have to create new characters and new events. Sometimes only a title is saved.

Paddy Chayefsky spoke about adapting a film from a play:

> "A play is manifestly different from a screenplay. You've got a stage, a proscenium; you've got an audience sitting there that knows it's in a theater. They are willing to accept all kinds of conventions that go with the theater. It's a different discipline, almost a different genre." (Interview with John Brady quoted in *The Craft of the Screenwriter*.)

Cross-plot

A cross-plot is a diagrammed reflection of a screenplay, designed to group scenes in shooting order, taking into account locations, actors' schedules, and other elements. A cross-plot is not made by the scriptwriter, but he must know what it is in order to understand that a script is a blueprint for making a film. If a script cannot be cross-plotted and budgeted, it cannot be produced and directed.

By using a "production board" (a large fold-out notebook mounted with thin strips, each of which is movable and represents a particular scene), the cross-plot becomes the key element in the creation of an efficient shooting schedule. Each scene is designated on an individual strip, which contains vital information such as shot number, actors involved in the scene, time (day or night), stunt or vehicle requirements, location, and a short description of the action. Again, the strips are movable, enabling the production manager and the director to lay out each day's shooting prior to filming.

Because filmmaking is an elaborate, expensive process requiring many technicians and cumbersome equipment, efficiency demands that all scenes that take place at a given location be shot at one time. Although this usually precludes shooting a film in the sequence in which it was written, considerable time and, thus, money are saved. For instance, an actor may be needed for three separate scenes each thirty script pages apart. Unless his scenes were scheduled for shooting closely together, that particular actor would have to be kept on salary for virtually the entire filming. Similarly, the use of a nonstudio location may pose a problem. If, for example, a mansion is to be used and it is only available for a week, all the scenes in that location have to be scheduled for that week, regardless of where they fall in the script. A cross-plot allows a director and production manager to make the most efficient use of their resources.

Storyboards

Storyboards are made by sketch artists in the preproduction months before shooting begins. They help the director, cameraman, set designers, and others to visualize key scenes and to save valuable production time. If the script is in the proper form and carries all of the relevant description, the director and sketch artist together can easily visualize what is going to be shown on the screen.

CHAPTER 10

The Business of Filmmaking

The making of motion pictures is at once an industry, a craft, and an art. The scriptwriter is merely one of the team who will make the film. He rarely does the whole job alone. He participates in art-by-committee. While the writer is free to write whatever he likes, he has a better chance of success if he understands the basic economics of filmmaking, the costs of production, trends in the market, and the audience he is writing for among producers and the public.

Film as industry

Film is one of the two most expensive art forms, architecture being the other. Therefore, in order to justify its costs in the American free enterprise system, a film must be designed to entertain a mass audience. If a film made by a studio or an independent producer does not earn back its investment plus a profit, it is a failure, regardless of critical reception. The failure of the single film *Heaven's Gate* in 1980 wiped out one of the oldest production companies, United Artists, whose stock was bought up by MGM.

The cost of filmmaking has grown so rapidly that in almost every other country in the world, the government subsidizes the domestic film industry and often helps to finance foreign films produced with domestic facilities and employing domestic technical crews. The American film industry now produces only about two hundred feature films a year compared to over four hundred during the Great Depression. The turnover in the movie houses averaged three films a week (or six with double-features) then, compared to less than one a week today. Those who created the film industry and established the big studios were themselves filmmakers and controlled every aspect of production. Today's filmmaking is controlled by business conglomerates such as Gulf & Western, Kinney, MGM Hotel, U. S. Steel, Quaker Oats, Mattel Toys, and *Reader's Digest*, to name just a few who have bought up studios as an investment.

To break even, a film must make back three times the cost of the negative. This means that few important decisions about a film are left to the discretion of those who make the film. Scripts are bought because someone thinks he can make money on them. No one sets out to make a money-losing theatrical film. The writer should write the best script he can but be conscious of production conditions and costs.

Film as craft

Craftsmanship, sometimes derided as "slickness," is the mark of American films. The fact is that technical proficiency in sound recording, lighting, editing, cinematography, and special effects is the hallmark of the American film, sustained by strong unions and standards.

Film as art

The idea that a script is a work of art is the idea of an amateur. A script is a blueprint for making a film. By itself, it is neither literature nor art. The filmscript that is a literary work of art is about as common as the architect's blueprint that is hung in a museum. Film art depends on the talents of all who participate in the making of the film. The writer's contribution to the team is a good script.

A good script is one with a theme of contemporary and universal significance, with vivid characters revealed through action, with glamor and theatricality, and one which is well structured and well written. This was the standard of Shakespeare, of O'Neill, and of Goethe, who, as director of the court

94

theater of the duchy of Saxe-Weimar-Eisenach, said he would never produce a play, no matter how much he admired it, if it would not please an audience.

Kitsch. There is no exact English equivalent for this German word, but a close approximation is "manufactured entertainment" (not "trash" or "bad taste," which is the definition commonly assumed). Even so, kitsch has often risen above its level to become a work of art. The reasons for this are not clear; the dividing line is vague. Certainly, *The African Queen* and *Treasure of Sierra Madre* achieved more artistry than was foreseen by those who made the film. Most films are kitsch.

Exploitation films. Some producers deliberately make exploitation films: films that exploit the public's salacious interest in sex, violence, or a current event or scandal of significance. The writer still must do the best job he can do of that or any other film, regardless of the elements of sexploitation or exploitation.

Censorship. In the United States, there is no government censorship of films; there is no industry censorship of films: Nothing is banned. A producer may make anything he wants, no matter how vulgar, violent, or inflammatory, if he can find financing and distribution for it. Screenplays are protected by the First Amendment to the Constitution, which guarantees freedom of speech and expression.

The Motion Picture Association of America (MPAA) administers the Classification and Rating Administration (CARA), but is not a part of it. Three organizations form its governing Policy Review Committee: the National Association of Theater Owners (NATO), the Independent Film Importers and Distributors Association (IFIDA), and the MPAA. Richard D. Heffner, chairman of CARA since 1974, is not an industry person. CARA is composed of another six non-industry persons (all parents) whose sole aim and concern is to classify the films submitted to it—reasonably, fairly, and intelligently—as a service to parents who want a reliable guide to the suitability of films for viewing by children up to age 17. Nothing is "approved" or "disapproved," just classified:

G: General Audiences, all ages admitted.

PG: Parental guidance suggested. Some material may not be suitable for children.

PG-13: Parents are strongly cautioned to give special guidance for children under 13. Some material may be inappropriate for young children.

R: Restricted; under 17s require accompanying parent or adult guardian.

X: No one under age 17 admitted.

Rights of the writer. Under the CARA classification system, the rights of the creative individual, as well as the rights of the majority of parents, are respected. No writer or producer is required to change the content of his film. Producers voluntarily submit their films for rating and pay a fee for the services of CARA. However, it is not necessary to have a picture rated in order to get it exhibited; it is the exhibitors and their customers who want the rating as a guide. Many producers will choose to have a film re-edited to secure a lower rating that may open a larger market to them. There is an independent Appeals Board. Any producer has the right to appeal the rating judgment of CARA.

A good writer is aware his viewers are both refined in taste and raw in taste. Much of modern respectability, when imposed on the arts, is a form of blindness. It does not admit William Shakespeare's view of the audience's "irresponsible delight in vigorous events," which is more and more demonstrated in current films.

Opportunities for writers in the film industry

Writing is possibly the very best point of entry for one aspiring to be in filmmaking. The writer can produce by himself a product that can be shown and sold to networks, studios, and producers, who are always in need of talented writers. He has a strong advocate and representative in the Writers Guild of

America (East and West Coast branches), and admission is open to him after his first theatrical film sale. (See Appendix A, *Writers Guild of America: Functions and Services*.)

The newcomer should be aware of other kinds of employment for scriptwriters in which he can hone his skills and earn a living: television dramatic and comedy series, features, miniseries and documentaries, video cassettes, and pay cable. Industrial, business, political, military, propaganda, and science films made for education and training as well as publicity and promotion make up a multibillion-dollar-a-year industry that is growing fast.

Eleven hundred colleges and universities are now offering film courses. A great many of these courses are in film history and criticism. More and more schools are offering degrees in film production. Very often a trained scriptwriter with some film credits will be hired to teach scriptwriting, even if he doesn't have the advanced college degrees required in other academic disciplines.

Studios and independent producers employ *story analysts* or *editors* to read scripts, novels, plays, and short stories that are submitted to them. Story editors are usually experienced writers with special qualifications who are hired to find good scripts and stories. Producers depend on their story analysts to read whatever is submitted, synopsize each piece, recommend for or against acquiring the property, and make suggestions for changes. (See *Sample Topsheet and Synopsis* in Chapter 9.)

Options

Most writers will accept an offer of a three-month, six-month, or one-year option on a script, for which a small amount is paid up front by the would-be producer, who hopes to get someone else—a bank or a studio—to finance the production. If the picture is not made, all rights revert to the writer.

The screenwriter must contact the publisher and the original author's agent to negotiate an option to adapt someone else's novel, short story, or stage play. Occasionally a writer or producer fails to realize he must pay for an option on a property he wants to buy or adapt. This can be a serious mistake.

If the adaptation is sold without first securing the rights to the original property, the author and/or owner of the rights can sue and/or demand an exorbitant fee for the rights. Jerry Lewis made a film *(The Day the Clown Stopped Laughing)* that cannot be released because he failed to negotiate the rights to the story before he went into production. The writer was dissatisfied with the way her story was adapted and has refused to sell the rights to her original story. Had he paid for the rights before filming, she would have no claims against the adaptation. (See *Adaptations* in Chapter 9.) Securing permission from living people to portray them in a film is also the responsibility of the writer. Sometimes a newspaper headline or article suggests a good script idea. If the major characters are dead, it is still necessary to secure permission from surviving relatives if they will be depicted in the film.

Writers' rights

The Writers Guild negotiates minimum pay scales and conditions of work for screenwriters. This is called the Minimum Basic Agreement (MBA) and is signed by every producer. Agents may negotiate fees higher than the MBA calls for, as well as a percentage of the profits for the writer or a fixed deferred amount. The minimum payment must be "up front." (See Appendix A, *Writers Guild of America: Functions and Services.*)

It has been said that Broadway is a writer's medium and Hollywood a director's, partly because in a Dramatists Guild MBA, the playwright has final control of the script in production. No one can change the script without his permission. On the other hand, a motion picture script sale includes all rights and the scriptwriter retains no rights after payment.

In practice, few directors have "final cut" authority either, if this conflicts with studio executives' or financiers' demands.

Working on "spec"

Beginners can be easily suckered into speculating. *Never* agree to write something for nothing. Such a proposal is *not* "an opportunity to break in." Not even an outline or treatment should be given to a producer or director *at his request* without a contract that spells out what is to be paid the writer for each step as specified by the WGA-MBA.

Type-casting

It is common practice for story editors to categorize writers, perhaps on the basis of one successful script, as a Western writer, mystery, comedy, sci-fi, detective, historical drama, musical comedy, juveniles, romantic, war, psychological drama, etc. Whether this works to the writer's advantage or disadvantge is something only he can decide. Most competent professional writers can write any or all of the above.

The same kind of nonsense pertains to plot patterns. "So-and-so can write a love pattern," success pattern, Cinderella pattern, quest or return pattern, vengeance pattern, etc. Professional writers know that a story is a story and the difference is in how it is told. *Hamlet* was one of dozens of revenge stories popular in its day.

Agents

Are agents necessary?

Yes.

Both agents and the Writers Guild protect the writers' interests and are worth their costs; they work *for* the writer. Agents invest time and effort and their expertise in the writer, sometimes for a long time before it pays off.

A writer who is a "Scheherazade" (a superb storyteller) may do a good selling job in a story conference, but he should *never* represent himself in negotiations and never discuss terms of payment with the person for whom he will be working. If the writer makes a personal contact with someone interested in his script or services, he should inform his agent at once and not let him be surprised by hearing it from a third party.

Many writers initiate their own deals through personal contacts, but the contract should *always* be negotiated by an agent. All studios and producing companies have "boiler-plate" contracts, a basic contract which meets the Guild minimums, but such contracts are written to the producer's advantage, not the writer's. An agent may negotiate better payments, modify terms, or demand changes; a writer may not know what he is entitled to.

How to choose an agent. As in many other working relationships, word of mouth and personal recommendations and reputations carry weight. Appendix B is a current list of agents who have signed agreements with the WGA; this means that they will abide by all Guild rules in writing contracts for their clients. They cannot negotiate a contract for the writer for employment or sale of a screenplay, a script for a television series, pilot, miniseries, outline, treatment, option, residuals, pensions, or anything else covered by the WGA, for less than the MBA terms.

Note that some agents will not read any unsolicited material submitted to them. Some will only read material recommended to them by someone they know. Others will accept and read unsolicited material. This last category is the one for the novice to investigate with a query and sample script. The script form should follow *all* of the recommendations in Chapter 7. A script should be submitted loose, not bound. If he agrees to represent it, the agent will put his own distinctive cover on the script for identification.

What to expect of an agent. There are big agencies, small agencies, and some independent agents. Each type has its advantages and disadvantages. A big agency with dozens of agents and hundreds of clients may have more contacts in the industry, giving it greater clout. If it also represents directors, producers, and stars, and packages film projects, it may be able to secure employment for its writers on these projects and through these people. On the other hand, the new, unknown writer can get lost in a big agency. His script may be forever at the bottom of the pile.

An independent agent or small agency with a shorter list of clients may work harder for the newcomer. Hollywood generally worships youth and newness and will welcome the young newcomer who can deliver the old, tried-and-true formula story.

Scripts can be registered with WGA for a small fee (see Appendix A). However, submission of a script by an agent also protects the writer. Agents keep records of submissions, so producers are not likely to steal ideas.

It is very unusual for a script to be stolen, and even rarer for a suit for plagiarism to succeed. A suit for plagiarism requires proving more than two or three incidents in common. Most plagiarism of lines or brief episodes is unconscious and unintended. It is unimportant whether a *theme* has been used before. What is important is what story is hung on it. Rerunning ideas in new forms is popular. Thus, the Japanese film *Seven Samurai* became the Western, *The Magnificent Seven*, and the Japanese *Yojimbo* became the first "Spaghetti Western," *A Fistful of Dollars*.

The agent should read the script before sending it out. He may correct errors of grammar, spelling, or fact (which should not be necessary). He may offer *suggestions* for changes, but do not let him rewrite or even demand a rewrite unless you agree with his ideas. If the agent is too busy to read the scripts and says "just tell me the story," he will probably be too busy to sell it.

Collaboration

WGA has a basic collaboration agreement protecting the rights of all parties. Writers entering into a collaboration with one or more partners should be aware in advance of the problem of what to do if an offer is made for a jointly written script and one partner wishes to accept the offer and the other wishes to reject it. The one who wants to reject must buy out the one who wants to accept. Thus, one partner cannot do the other out of a potential sale by holding out.

The importance of the screenwriter

Filmmaking is mankind's newest and most popular art and entertainment form. It has universal appeal and a worldwide market. Whatever appears on the screen is the result of the screenwriter's idea and vision, executed by many people. The writer with talent and imagination, who learns his craft and the business that employs it, has an important role in filmmaking and will always command respect.

Writers Guild of America: Functions and Services

GUILD FUNCTIONS AND SERVICES

1. CONTRACTS
   a. Negotiation of Basic Agreements in screen, television (live, tape, and film), radio, and staff agreements (news and continuity writers).
   b. Administration of same:
      (1) Handling of writer claims.
      (2) Checking of individual writer contracts for Minimum Basic Agreement (MBA) violations.
      (3) Enforcement of working rules.
      (4) Processing of grievances.
      (5) Arbitrations under the MBA.
      (6) Collection and processing of television and motion picture residuals.
      (7) Pension plan.
      (8) Health and welfare plan.

2. CREDITS
   a. Receipt of tentative notices.
   b. Arbitration of protests.
   c. Maintenance of credit records.
   d. Distribution of credits manual.
   e. Credit information to members and to producers and agents.

3. ORIGINAL MATERIAL
   a. Registration service.
   b. Collaboration agreements.
   c. Settlement of disputes (Committee on Original Material).
   d. Copyright information and legislation.

4. AGENTS
   a. Negotiation of Basic Agreement with agents.
   b. Recording, filing, and administration of individual agreements between writers and agents.
   c. Distribution of lists of authorized agents.
   d. Arbitration function in disputes between writers and agents.

5. EMPLOYMENT
   a. Compilation and distribution of TV market lists.
   b. Compilation and circulation of motion picture and TV credits lists to producers and agents.
   c. Compilation and circulation of statistical data re members where requested.

6. INFORMATION
   a. Inquiries by producers re member credits, agents, and contract provisions.
   b. Inquiries by members and non-members re production data and contract provisions.

7. AFFILIATION AND COOPERATION
   a. Writers Guild of Great Britain.
   b. Australian Writers Guild.
   c. Association of Canadian Television and Radio Artists (ACTRA).
   d. Motion Picture and Television Relief Fund.
   e. Permanent Charities Committee.
   f. American Film Institute.
   g. Affirmative Action program.
   h. Other industry functions and services.

8. PUBLIC RELATIONS
   a. Publications—Newsletter.
   b. Trade press.
   c. TV forums.
   d. Annual awards event.

9. CREDIT UNION
   a. Loans.
   b. Investments.
   c. Life insurance.

10. GROUP INSURANCE
    a. Life insurance.
    b. Disability; Hospitalization; Major medical.

11. LEGISLATION
    a. Copyright.
    b. Censorship.
    c. Taxation.
    d. Unemployment compensation.

12. FILM SOCIETY

13. WORKSHOP PROGRAMS

14. SUPPORT OF FREEDOM OF EXPRESSION
    a. Litigation.
    b. Press.
    c. Other.

15. DIRECTORY

16. COMMITTEES
    a. Writer conferences.
    b. Social activities.

17. WRITERS GUILD THEATER
    a. Screenings. (See *Film Society.*)
    b. Rental.

Information Sheet for Admission to the WGA

The WGA represents writers primarily for the purpose of collective bargaining in its jurisdiction of screen, television, and radio.

Membership entrance requirements are two (2) or more employments for writing services *or* sales of literary material *or* term *or* week-to-week employment; *or* a single employment for a theatrical screenplay, *or* two-hour teleplay, *or* two-hour radio play, *or* ninety (90) minute story and teleplay *or* ninety (90) minute story and radio play in the Guild's jurisdiction for an aggregate of twelve (12) Units of Credit as established by the WGA Constitution and Bylaws as amended July 28, 1983. A copy of the Units of Credit Schedule follows. All employment or sales must have been during the two (2) years preceding application for membership and must be with a company or other entity that is signatory to the applicable WGA collective bargaining agreement.

The initiation fee of $1,500.00 is payable only by Cashier's Check or by Money Order. All membership applications are to be supported by a copy of executed employment or sales contracts or other acceptable evidence of employment or sales.

The WGA does not obtain employment or sales for writers nor do we refer or recommend members for writing assignments. It does not accept, evaluate, or handle material for submission. Literary material should be submitted to a production company or through a literary agent.

The Television Market List, featuring contact and submission information on current weekly prime-time television programs, is published monthly (except July and August) in the *WGA Newsletter* and is available to non-members at $2.50 (Two Dollars Fifty Cents) per issue or $20.00 (Twenty Dollars) for a yearly subscription. Send your request with a check or money order to the *WGA Newsletter*, 8955 Beverly Blvd., Los Angeles, CA 90048.

The WGA does not offer writing instruction or advice. For this information, communicate with film schools, the state colleges, universities, or with your local Board of Education.

Guild policy does not allow the WGA to disclose the address or phone number of any Guild member. First Class correspondence may be addressed to a member in care of the Guild and will be promptly forwarded to members without a referral address such as an agent. Please contact the Agency Department for further information.

A helpful booklet to the accepted script format entitled PROFESSIONAL WRITER'S TELEPLAY/SCREENPLAY GUIDE is available through *Writers Guild East*. The cost is $2.50 and the address is 555 West 57th Street, New York, NY 10019.

Schedule of Units of Credit

Writers Guild of America Constitution and By-Laws
Article IV. Section 3, as amended 7-28-83

If a person is employed within the Guild's jurisdiction on a week-to-week or term basis he shall be entitled to one Unit of Credit for each complete week of such employment.

Units of Credit may also be obtained in accordance with the following schedule:

ONE UNIT

A series for which writer received "Created by" credit, **or**
Comedy-Variety Program: one unit per week of employment or
one unit per show, whichever is more.

TWO UNITS

Story for theatrical motion picture short subject, **or**
Story for TV or radio program one-half hour or less.

THREE UNITS

Screenplay for theatrical motion picture short subject, **or**
Teleplay or radio play for program one-half hour or less, **or**
Television format or presentation for a new series.

FOUR UNITS

Story for one-hour TV or radio program.

FIVE UNITS

Story and teleplay or story and radio play one-half hour or less.

SIX UNITS

Story for 90-minute teleplay or radio play, **or**
One-hour teleplay or radio play, **or**
Comedy-variety special regardless of length.

EIGHT UNITS

Story for theatrical motion picture, **or**
Story for two-hour TV or radio program.

NINE UNITS

90-minute teleplay or radio play.

TEN UNITS

One-hour story and teleplay or story and radio play.

TWELVE UNITS

The following shall constitute two employments or sales and 12
units:
Screenplay for theatrical motion picture, **or**
Two-hour teleplay or two-hour radio play, **or**
90-minute story and teleplay or story and radio play.

Please note:

A rewrite is entitled to one-half the number of units allotted to its
particular category.

A polish is entitled to one-quarter the number of units allotted to its particular category.

Where writers collaborate on the same project each shall be accorded the appropriate number of units for its category.

WRITERS GUILD REGISTRATION SERVICE	WRITERS GUILD OF AMERICA, WEST, INC. 8955 BEVERLY BOULEVARD LOS ANGELES, CA 90048-2456 PHONE: *Registration* 213 205-2500 *General Information* 213 550-1000
PURPOSE	The Guild's Registration Service has been set up to assist members and non-members in establishing the completion date and the identity of their literary property written for the fields of theatrical motion pictures, television, and radio.
VALUE	Registration does not confer any statutory protection. It merely provides evidence of the writer's claim to authorship of the literary material involved and of the date of its completion. A writer has certain rights under the law the moment the work is completed. It is therefore important that the date of completion be legally established. The Registration Office does not make comparisons of registration deposits to determine similarity between works, nor does it give legal opinions or advice.
COVERAGE	Since the value of registration is merely to supply evidence, it cannot protect what the law does not protect. Registration with the Guild does not protect titles (neither does registration with the United States Copyright Office).
PROCEDURE FOR DEPOSIT	One (1) 8½ x 11 unbound (no brads, staples, etc.) copy is required for deposit in the Guild files. When it is received, the property is sealed in a Guild Registration Envelope, timed, and dated. A receipt is returned. Notice of registra-

108

tion shall consist of the following wording: REGISTERED WGAw NO._____ (the registration number will be on the receipt) and be applied upon the title page or the page immediately following. Scripts specifically intended for radio, television, and theatrical motion pictures, series formats, step outlines, and storylines are registrable. The Guild does not accept book manuscripts, stage plays, music, lyrics, photos, drawings, or articles of public record for filing. Each property must be registered separately (exception: three episodes, skits, or sketches for an existing series may be deposited as a single registration). Be sure that the name under which you register is your full legal name. The use of pseudonyms, pen names, initials, or familiar forms of a proper name may require proof of identity if you want to recover the material left on deposit.

FEES

$5.00 for members of WGAw and WGAe
$10.00 for non-members

THE FEE MUST ACCOMPANY THE MATERIAL THAT IS TO BE REGISTERED.

LOCATION OF REGISTRATION OFFICE

8955 BEVERLY BOULEVARD
LOS ANGELES, CA 90048
(corner of Almont Drive, one block east of Doheny Drive)

HOURS

10 A.M. to 12 NOON ⎫ MONDAY through
2 P.M. to 5 P.M. ⎬ FRIDAY

DURATION

Material deposited for registration after September 1, 1982 is valid for a term of five (5) years; material deposited for registration prior to September 1, 1982 is valid for a term of ten (10) years. You may renew the registration for an additional ten (10) year or five (5) year term, whichever is applicable, at the then current registration fee. You authorize the Guild to destroy the material without notice to you on the expiraton of the term of registration if renewal is not made. The fee should accompany the request for renewal.

PROCEDURE FOR WITHDRAWAL

The registered copy left on deposit cannot be returned to the writer without defeating the purpose of registration, the point being that evidence should be available, if necessary, that the material has been in the Guild's charge since the date of deposit.

However, if the writer finds it necessary to have the copy returned, at least forty-eight (48) hours' notice of intended withdrawal must be given to the Guild. A manuscript will be given up only on the signature(s) of the writer(s). If the registration is in the names of more than one person, the written consent of all is required to authorize withdrawal. In case a registrant is deceased, proof of death and the consent of his representative or heirs must be presented. In no event, except under these provisions, shall any of the material be allowed to be taken from the Guild office unless a court order has been acquired.

If any person other than the writer named in the registration shall request confirmation of registration, the registration number and/or date of deposit, to see either the material deposited, the registration envelope, or any other material, such request shall be denied unless authorization from the writer(s) or a court order is presented in connection therewith.

COPYRIGHT   The Guild does not have a copyright service. For forms and instructions call: 202 287-9100.

Blanche W. Baker
Registration Administrator

9/16/85

Used by permission, Writers Guild of America.

APPENDIX B

———

Writers Guild Agency List

Reproduced courtesy of the Writers Guild of America, West, Inc., 8955 Beverly Boulevard, Los Angeles, CA 90048; current as of January 1, 1986. Copyright © 1986.

LA	—Los Angeles	NH	—North Hollywood
BH	—Beverly Hills	NY	—New York
Hwd	—Hollywood	SM	—Santa Monica
SC	—Studio City	SF	—San Francisco
SO	—Sherman Oaks	WH	—West Hollywood

All telephone numbers are Area Code 213
unless otherwise noted.

We suggest that the individual first write or telephone the agency, detail his professional and/or academic credentials, and briefly describe the nature of the material he desires to submit. The agency will then advise the individual whether it is interested in receiving the material with a view toward representing it.

Most agencies, as a courtesy to writers, will return material sent to them if a self-addressed stamped envelope accompanies the submission. However, should a submission not be returned for any reason, the individual should be aware that the agency is under no obligaton to return literary material to a writer seeking representation. The Guild cannot assist in seeking the return of material.

We regret we can offer no assistance in finding, selecting, or recommending an agent.

(*)   This agency has indicated that it will consider unsolicited material from writers.

(**) This agency has indicated that it will consider unsolicited material from writers only as a result of references from persons known to it.

(P)   Indicates packaging agency.

(S)   Society of Authors Representatives—signed through WGA only.

The following agencies have subscribed to the Writers Guild of America-Artists' Manager Basic Agreement to 1976:

*Act 48 Mgmt., 1501 Broadway, #705, NY (10036), 212 354-4250

Adams Limited, Bret, 448W. 44th St., NY (10036), 212 765-5630

**Agency For The Performing Arts (P), 9000 Sunset Bl., #1200, LA (90069), 273-0744

Agency For The Performing Arts (P), 888 7th Ave., NY (10016), 212 582-1500

**Altoni, Buddy, PO Box 1022, Newport Beach, CA (92663), 714 851-1711

*Amsterdam Agency, Marcia, 41 W. 82nd St., #9A, NY (10024), 212 873-4945

**Applegate & Assoc., A & A, 1633 Vista Del Mar, #201, LA (90028), 818 240-9700

Artists Agency, The (P), 10000 Santa Monica Bl., #305, LA (90067), 277-7779

Associated Artists Mgmt., 1501 Broadway, #1808A, NY (10036), 212 398-0460

**Assoc. Talent International, 9744 Wilshire Bl., #360, BH (90212), 271-4662

*A Total Acting Experience, 6736 Laurel Canyon Bl., #323, NH (91606), 818 765-7244

**Authors & Artists Agency, 4444 Lakeside Dr., Burbank, CA (91505), 818 845-4500

**Barracliffe Agency, 2450 Americas Tower, LB129, 2323 Bryan St., Dallas, TX (75201), 214 979-0900

Barskin Agency, The, 11240 Magnolia Bl., #201, NH (91601), 818 985-2992

Baskins Agency, 293 Central Park W., #6F, NY (10024), 212 362-5667

**Bauer Agency, Martin, 9255 Sunset Bl., #710, LA (90069), 275-2421

Beakel & Jennings Agency, 427 N. Canon Dr., #205, BH (90210), 274-5418

**Beaty Agency, Mike, 1350 Manufacturing St., #217, Dallas, TX (75207), 214 747-8880

*Beckett Agency, The Russell, 5212 Colefax Ave., NH (91607), 666-8182

**Bennett Agency, The, 150 S. Barrington, #1, LA (90049), 471-2251

Berger Assoc., Bill (S), 444 E. 58th St., NY (10022), 212 486-9588

Berman, Lois, 240 W. 44th St., NY (10036)

Bernstein, Ron, 119 W. 57th St., NY (10019), 212 265-0750

Big Red Talent Ent., 8330 Third St., LA (90048), 874-5827

Blassingame, McCauley & Wood (S), 60 E. 42nd St., NY (10017)

**Bloom, Levy, Shorr & Assoc., 800 S. Robertson Bl., LA (90035), 659-6160

Bloom, Harry, 8833 Sunset Bl., #202, LA (9009), 659-5985

Bloom, J. Michael, 400 Madison Ave., 20th Fl., NY (10017), 212 832-6900

Bloom, J. Michael, 9200 Sunset Bl., #1210, LA (90069), 275-6800

Blue Star Agency, PO Box 2754, Arlington, VA (22202)

**Borinstein, Mark, 8600 Melrose Ave., LA (90069), 658-8094

*Braintree Prod., 422 E. 81st St., NY (10028), 212 472-2451

Brandon & Assoc., Paul, 9046 Sunset Bl., LA (90069), 273-6173

Breitner Literary Assoc., Susan, 1650 Broadway, #501, NY (10019)

Brewis Agency, Alex, 8721 Sunset Bl., LA (90069), 274-9874

**Broder-Kurland-Webb, 8439 Sunset Bl., #402, LA (90069), 656-9262

Brody Agency, The, PO Box 291423, Davie, FL (33329), 305 473-1770

Brooke-Dunn-Oliver, 9165 Sunset Bl., #202, LA (90069), 859-1405

Brown Agency, J., 8733 Sunset Bl., #102, LA (90069), 550-0296

Brown, Ltd., Curtis, Ten Astor Pl., NY (10003), 212 473-5400

Brown, Ned, 407 N. Maple Dr., BH (90210), 276-1131

**Browne Ltd., Pema, 185 E. 85th St., NY (10028), 212 369-1925

*BTV Ltd., PO Box 460, NY (10016), 212 696-5469

Buchwald & Assoc., Don, 10 E. 44th St., NY (10017), 212 867-1070

*Butler, Ruth, 8622 Reseda Bl., #211, Northridge, CA (91324), 818 886-8440

**Canyon State Career Mgmt., PO Box 41512, Phoenix, AZ (85080), 602 581-9282

Career Mgmt., 435 S. La Cienega Bl., #108, LA (90048), 657-1020

*Carpenter Co., 1434-6th Ave., San Diego, CA (92101), 619 235-8482

Carroll Agency, William, 448 N. Golden Mall, Burbank, CA (91502), 818 848-9948

Carvainis Agency, Maria, 235 West End Ave., NY (10023), 212 580-1559

**Case, Bertha, 345 W. 58th St., NY (10019), 212 541-9451

**Cavaleri & Assoc., 6605 Hollywood Bl., #220, Hwd (90028), 461-2940

Chandler Agency, The, 3123 Cahuenga Bl. W., LA (90068), 857-0787

Charter Mgmt., 9000 Sunset Bl., #1112, LA (90069), 278-1690

Chasman & Strick, Assoc., 6725 Sunset Bl., #506, Hwd (90028), 463-1115

*Chiz Agency, Terry H., 5761 Whitnall Hwy., #E, NH (91061), 818 506-0994

*Cinema Talent Agency, 7906 Santa Monica Bl., #209, LA (90046), 656-1937

**Clients Agency, 8600 Melrose Ave., LA (90069), 659-9999

Colton, Kingsley & Assoc., 16661 Ventura Bl., #400, Encino, CA (91436), 818 788-6043

Connell & Assoc., Polly, 4605 Lankershim Bl., NH (91602), 818 985-6266

*Consulting Concepts, 566 E. Chelsea Dr., Bountiful, UT (84010), 801 298-7373

Contemporary-Korman Artists, 132 Lasky Dr., BH (90212), 278-8250

**Conway & Assoc., Ben, 999 N. Doheny Dr., LA (90069), 271-8133

**Coppage Co., The, 9046 Sunset Bl., #201, LA (90069), 273-6173

**Coralie Jr., Agency, 4789 Vineland Ave., #100, NH (91602), 818 766-9501

Creative Artists Agency (P), 1888 Century Park E., LA (90067), 277-4545

Cumber Attractions, Lil, 6515 Sunset Bl., Hwd (90028), 469-1919

Dade/Rosen Assoc., 9172 Sunset Bl. #2, LA (90069), 278-7077

*de la Cerda & Assoc., Destiny, 5618 Post Rd., NY (10471), 212 796-6540

Dennis, Karg, Dennis and Co., 470 S. San Vicente Bl., LA (90048), 651-1700

*DeVane Interventions, 11030 Ventura Bl., #1-BB, SC (91604), 818 509-9339

Diamant, Anita (S), 51 E. 42nd St., NY (10017)
**Diamond Artists, 9200 Sunset Bl., #909, LA (90069), 278-8146
Donadio & Assoc., Candida (S), 111 W. 57th St., NY (10019), 212 757-7076
**Dorese Agency, Alyss Barlow, 41 W. 82nd St., NY (10024), 212 580-2855
**Dworski & Assoc., 9046 Sunset Bl., LA (90069), 273-6173

*Elizabeth IV Agency, 16200 Ventura Bl., #218-B, Encino, CA (91436), 818 789-9109
Elmo Agency, Ann (S), 60 E. 42nd St., NY (10165), 212 661-2880
**Evans & Assoc., Rick, PO Box 1393, Crystal Bay, NV (89402)

Fallon Agency, Diane, 5 Dickens Ct., Irvine, CA (92715), 714 955-0121
Ferrell Agency, Carol, 818 708-7773
*Ferris Agency, 5850 Canoga Ave., #110, Woodland Hills, CA (91367)
**Field Agency, The Maggie, 12725 Ventura Bl., #D, SC (91604), 818 980-2001
Fischer Co., Sy (P), 1 E. 57th St., NY (10022), 212 486-0426
Fox Chase Agency (S), 419 E. 57th St., NY (10022), 212 752-8211
Freedman Agency, Robert A., 1501 Broadway, #2310, NY (10036) 212 840-5760
*Freyman, Evelyn, 1660 L St., N.W., #1000, Washington, D.C. (20036) 202 775-1041
Frings Agency, Kurt, 415 S. Crescent Dr., #320, BH (90210), 274-8881

Garon-Brooke Assoc., Jay, 415 Central Park W., 15th Fl., NY (10025), 212 866-3654
*Garrick International Agency, Dale, 8831 Sunset Bl., LA (90069), 657-2661
Geddes Agency, 8749 Holloway Dr., LA (90069), 657-3392
**Gelff Assoc., Laya, 16000 Ventura Bl., #500, Encino, CA (91436), 818 906-0925
**Gerard, Paul, 2918 Alta Vista, Newport Beach, CA (92660), 714 644-7950
**Gerritsen International, 8721 Sunset Bl., #203, LA (90069), 659-8414
Gersh Agency, Inc., The, 222 N. Canon Dr., BH (90210), 274-6611

Gibson Agency, J. Carter, 9000 Sunset Bl., #811, LA (90069), 274-8813

**Gilbert, Jay, 8400 Sunset Bl., #3-d, LA (90069), 656-8090

**GMA, 1741 N. Ivar St., #221, Hwd (90028), 466-7161

**Gold Dust Talent Agency, 207 S. Western Bl., #209, LA (90004), 739-0908

Goldstein & Assoc., Allen, 900 Sunset Bl., #1105, LA (90069), 278-5005

Grashin Agency, Mauri, 8170 Beverly Bl., #109, LA (90048), 651-1828

**Gray Agency, Stephen, 9025 Wilshire Bl., #309, BH (90211), 550-7000

Green Agency, Ivan, The, 9911 W. Pico Bl., #1490, LA (90035), 277-1541

**Greene, Harold R., 760 N. La Cienega Bl., LA (90069), 855-0824

Groffsky Literary Agency, Maxine, 2 Fifth Ave., NY (10011), 212 677-2720

Grossman & Assoc., Larry, 211 S. Beverly Dr., #206, BH (90212), 550-8127

Hamilburg Agency, Mitchell, 292 S. La Cienega Bl., BH (90211), 657-1501

Hashagen & Assoc., Rick, 157 W. 57th St., NY (10019), 212 315-3130

**Heacock Literary Agency, Inc., 1523 6th St., SM (90401), 393-6227

**Henderson/Hogan Agency, 247 S. Beverly Dr., BH (90212), 274-7815

Henderson/Hogan Agency, 200 W. 57th St., NY (10019), 212 765-5190

**Hesseltine/Baker Assoc., 165 W. 46th St., #409, NY (10036) 212 921-4460. Letters only.

*Hoffman, Harriet K., PO Box 26071, Ft. Lauderdale, FL (33320), 305 721-9283

**Hunt Mgmt., Diana, 44 W. 44th St., #1414, NY (10036), 212 391-4971

Hunt & Assoc., George, 8350 Santa Monica Bl., LA (90069), 654-6600

International Creative Mgmt. (P), 8899 Beverly Bl., LA (90048), 550-4000

International Creative Mgmt. (P), 40 W. 57th St., NY (10019), 212 556-5600

International Literary Agents, 9000 Sunset Bl., #1115, LA (90069), 874-2563

*International Talent Agency, 6253 Hollywood Bl., #230, Hwd (90028) 461-4901

Ippolito, Andrew, 4 E. 46th St., NY (10017), 212 687-0404

*Jaffe Representatives, 140 7th Ave., #2L, NY (10011), 212 741-1359

**Jaynese, Janis, PO Box 646, Wolfforth, TX (79382), 806 866-4941

**Jefferson & Ellis, 8383 Wilshire Bl., #1024, BH (90211), 655-1001

**Joseph/Knight Agency, 6331 Hollywood Bl., #924, Hwd (90028), 465-5474

Kane Agency, Merrily, 9171 Wilshire Bl. #300, BH (90210), 550-8874

Karlan Agency, Patricia, 4425 Riverside Dr., #102, Burbank, CA (91505) 818 846-8666

Katavolos Terenia, 300 E. 51st St., NY (10022). Query letters only.

*Kerwin Agency, Wm., 1605 N. Cahuenga Bl., #202, Hwd (90028), 469-5155

**Keynan-Goff Assoc., 2049 Century Park E., #4370, LA (90067), 556-0339

*King, Ltd., Archer, 1440 Broadway, #2100, NY (10018), 212 764-3905

*Kingsley Corp., 112 Barnsbee Ln., Coventry, CT (06238), 203 742-9575

**Kohner Agency, Paul (P), 9169 Sunset Bl., LA (90069), 550-1060

**Kopaloff Co., The, 1930 Century Park W., #303, LA (90067), 203-8430

Kroll Agency, Lucy (S), 390 West End Ave., NY (10024), 212 877-0627

Lazar, Irving Paul, 211 S. Beverly Dr., BH (90212), 275-6153

**Leading Artists, Inc., 445 N. Bedford Dr., Penthouse, BH (90210), 858-1999

*Lee Literary Agency, L. Harry, Box 203, Rocky Point, NY (11778), 516 744-1188. Letters only.

Lenny Assoc., Jack, 9701 Wilshire Bl., BH (90212), 271-2174

Lenny Assoc., Jack, 140 W. 58th St., NY (10019), 212 582-0272

Light Co., The, 113 N. Robertson Bl., LA (90048), 273-9602

Light Co., The, 1443 Wazee St., 3rd Fl., Denver, CO (80202), 303 572-8363

Literary Artists Mgmt., PO Box 1604, Monterey, CA (93940), 408 899-7145

*London Group Ltd., 505 5th Ave., #1602, NY (10017), 212 870-0713

Loo, Bessie, 8235 Santa Monica Bl., LA (90046), 650-1300

Lund Agency, The, 6515 Sunset Bl., #304, Hwd (90028), 466-8280

Lynne & Reilly Agency, 6290 Sunset Bl., #1002, Hwd (90028), 461-2828

Major Talent Agency (P), 11812 San Vicente Bl., #510, LA (90049), 820-5841

**Management One, Talent Agency, 6464 Sunst Bl., #590, Hwd (90028) 461-7515

*Manhattan Artists Co., 400 W. 40th St., NY (10018), 212 244-6931

**Mann Agency, Sheri, 11601 Dunstan Way, #309, LA (90049), 476-0177

Maris Agency, 17620 Sherman Way, #8, Van Nuys, CA (91406), 818 708-2493

Markson Literary Agency, Elaine, 44 Greenwich Ave., NY (10011), 212 243-8480

**Marshall Agency, The, 2330 Westwood Bl., #204, LA (90064), 650-1628

**Matson Co., Harold, 276 5th Ave., NY (10001), 212 679-4490

McCartt, Oreck, Barrett, 9200 Sunset Bl., #531, Hwd (90069), 278-6243

*McCormick Talent, 98-1247 Kaahumanu St., #310A, Aiea, HI (96701), 808 487-5456

Merit Agency, The, 12926 Riverside Dr., #C, SO (91423), 818 986-3017

Merrill, Helen, 361 W. 17th St., NY (10011), 212 691-5326

Messenger Agency, Fred, 8235 Santa Monica Bl., LA (90046), 654-3800

Meyer Agency, Peter (P), 9220 Sunset Bl., #303, LA (90069), 273-3303

Miller, Lee, 1680 N. Vine St., #417, Hwd (90028), 469-0077

**Mills, Ltd., Robert P., 333 5th Ave., NY (10016), 212 685-6575

Morris Agency, William (P), 151 El Camino Dr., BH (90212), 274-7451

Morris Agency, William (P), 1350 Ave. of the Americas, NY (10019), 212 586-5100
Morton Agency, 1105 Glendon Ave., LA (90024), 824-4089
**Moss, Marvin (P), 9200 Sunset Bl., LA (90069), 274-8483

**Nachtigall Agency, The, 1885 Lombard St., SF (94123), 415 346-1115
Neighbors, Charles, 240 Waverly Pl., NY (10014), 212 924-8296
New England Literary Agency, PO Box 240, Granville, NY (12832), 518 642-2629
**New World Artists, 8780 Sunset Bl., LA (90069), 659-9737

Ober & Assoc., Harold (S), 40 E. 49th St., NY (10017), 212 759-8600
Oscard Assoc., Fifi, 19 W. 44th St., NY (10022), 212 764-1100
*Overseas Artists Ltd, 1900 Ave. of the Stars, #290, LA (90069), 652-4899

*Panda Agency, 3721 Hoen Ave., Santa Rosa, CA (95405), 707 544-3671
Paramuse Artists Assoc., 1414 Ave. of the Americas, NY (10019), 212 758-5055
Phoenix Literary Agency, 531 E. 72nd St., NY (10021), 212 734-0403
**Pleshette Agency, Lynn, 2700 N. Beachwood Dr., Hwd (90068), 465-0428
**Preminger Agency, Jim (P), 1650 Westwood Bl., #201, LA (90024), 475-9491
Prescott Agency, Guy, The, 8920 Wonderland Ave., LA (90046), 656-1963

Raines & Raines, 71 Park Ave., NY (10016), 212 684-5160
Raper Enterprises Agency, 9441 Wilshire Bl., #620D, BH (90210), 273-7704
Rappa Agency, Ray, 7471 Melrose Ave., #11, LA (90046) 653-7000
**Regency Artists Ltd., 9200 Sunset Bl., #823, LA (90069), 273-7103
*Rhodes Literary Agency, 140 West End Ave., NY (10023), 212 580-1300. Letters only.
**Richland Agency, The, 1888 Century Park E., #1107, LA (90067), 553-1257

**Roberts Co., The, 427 N. Canon Dr., BH (90210), 275-9384
*Roberts, Flora, 157 W. 57th St., NY (10019), 212 355-4165
Robinson-Luttrell & Assoc., 141 El Camino Dr., #110, BH (90212), 275-6114
**Rogers & Assoc., Stephanie, 9100 Sunset Bl., #340, LA (90069), 278-2015
Rose Agency, Jack, 6430 Sunset Bl., #1203, Hwd (90028), 463-7300
Rupa Agency, Ray, 7471 Melrose Ave., #11, LA (90046), 653-7000

Safier, Gloria, 244 E. 53rd. St., NY (10022), 212 838-4868
**Sanders' Agency, Honey, 229 W. 42nd St., #404, NY (10036), 212 947-5555
**Sanders Agency, Norah, 1100 Glendon Ave., LA (90024), 824-2264
**S.F. Agency, 595 Mission St., #403, SF (94105), 415 495-5945
**Sanford-Beckett Agency, 1015 Gayley Ave., LA (90024), 208-2100
*Sanocki Agency, Sandy, 348 E. Olive, #K, Burbank, CA (91502), 818 840-8096
**Savage Agency, The, 6212 Banner Ave., LA (90038), 461-8316
*SBK Assoc., 11 Chamberlain, Waltham, MA (02154), 617 894-4037
**Scagnetti, Jack, 5330 Lankershim Bl., #210, NH (91601), 818 762-3871
**Schechter, Irv (P), 9300 Wilshire Bl., #410, BH (90212), 278-8070
*Schuster-Dowdell Org., The, PO Box 2, Valhalla, NY (10595) 914 761-3106
*Selected Artists Agency, 12711 Ventura Bl., #460, SC (91604), 818 763-9731. Query letters only.
**Selman, Edythea Ginis, Literary Agent, 14 Washington Pl., NY (10003), 212 473-1874
Shapira & Assoc., David, 15301 Ventura Blvd., #345, SO (91403), 818 906-0322
**Shaw Agency, Glenn, 3330 Barham Bl., Hwd (90068), 851-6262
Sherrell Agency, Lew, 7060 Hollywood Bl., Hwd (90028), 461-9955
**Shumaker Talent Agency, The, 10850 Riverside Dr., #410, NH (91609), 877-3370. Letters only.
*Sleeper Enterprises, 5016 Wright Terr., Skokie, IL (60077). Letters only.
**Smith Agency, Kimberly A., 10602 Stone Canyon Rd., #306, Dallas, TX (75230), 214 739-5407

Smith, Gerald K., PO Box 7430, Burbank, CA (91510), 849-5388

**Smith-Freedman & Assoc., 123 N. San Vicente Bl., BH (90211), 852-4777

**Steele & Assoc., Ellen Lively, PO Box 188, Organ, NM (88052), 505 382-5863

Stone-Masser Agency, 1052 Carol Dr., LA (90069), 275-9599

Suncoast Talent Agency, 422 S. Western Ave., LA (90020)

**Swanson, H. N., 8523 Sunset Bl., LA (90069), 652-5385

*Talent Group, The, 184 Bloor St., 4th Fl., E. Toronto, Ont. M4W 3J3, 416 961-3304

**Talent Network International, 9000 Sunset Bl., #807, LA (90069), 271-8403

Targ Literary Agency, Roslyn, 105 W. 13th St., NY (10011), 212 206-9390

Tel-Screen International, 7965 S.W. 146th St., Miami, FL (33158), 305 235-2722

**The Agency, 10351 Santa Monica Bl., #211, LA (90025), 551-3000

Tobias & Assoc., Herb, 1901 Ave. of the Stars, #840, LA (90067), 277-6211

*Townsend Agency, Jackie, 2600 Stemmons Fwy., #200, Dallas, TX (75207), 214 637-5700

**Triad Artists, 10100 Santa Monica Bl., 16th Fl., LA (90067), 556-2727

**Uffner & Assoc., Beth, 12725 Ventura Bl., SC (91604), 818 980-4500

**Universal Artists Agency, 9465 Wilshire Bl., #616, BH (90212), 278-2425

*Vamp Talent Agency, 713 E. La Loma Ave., #1, Somis, CA (93066), 805 485-2001

*Vass Talent Agency, 6404 Hollywood Bl., #428, LA (90028), 481-0263

*Wain Agency, Erika, 1418 N. Highland Ave., #102, Hwd (90028), 460-4224

Wallace & Sheil Agency (S), 177 E. 70th St., NY (10021), 212 570-9090

*Waugh Agency, Ann, 4731 Laurel Canyon Bl., #5, NH (91607), 818 980-0141

Wax & Associates, Elliott (P), 273-8217

Weiner & Assoc., 87 Horizon Terr., Hillsdale, NJ (07642), 201 664-9419

**Wendland, Jeffrey, CPA, 341 Music Ln., Grand Junction, CO (81501), 303 242-2549

*Wild Cats Studio, PO Box 85057, Las Vegas, NV (89185), 702 366-0553

**Wilder Agency, The, 8721 Sunset Bl., #101, LA (90069), 854-3521

**William Jeffreys Agency, 8455 Beverly Bl., #408, LA (90048), 651-3193

**Witzer Agency,Ted, 1900 Ave. of the Stars, #2850, LA (90067), 552-9521

Wormser, Heldfond & Joseph, 1717 N. Highland Ave., Hwd (90028), 466-9111

Wosk Agency, Sylvia, 439 S. La Cienega Bl., LA (90048), 274-8063

Wright Rep., Ann, 136 E. 57th St., NY (10022), 212 832-0110

**Wright, Marion A., 4317 Bluebell, SC (91604), 818 766-7307

**Wright Talent Agency, Carter, 6533 Hollywood Bl., #201, Hwd (90028), 469-0944

Writers & Artists Agency (P), 11726 San Vicente Bl., #300, LA (90049), 820-2240

Writers & Artists Agency (P), 162 W. 56th St., NY (10019), 212 246-9029

Writers Assoc. of N.Y., 915 Erie Bl., Syracuse, NY (13210), 315 474-6461

**Wunsch/Ostroff, 9220 Sunset Bl., #212, LA (90069), 278-1955

Wycoff & Assoc., 6331 Hollywood Bl., #1120, LA (90028), 464-4866

APPENDIX C

———

Sample Cross-Plot and Storyboards

Sample cross-plot, designed to reflect group scenes in shooting order, taking into account locations, actors' schedules, etc. If a script cannot be cross-plotted and budgeted, it cannot be produced and directed.

Sample storyboards from *The Sand Pebbles*. Reproduced with permission of Robert Wise Productions.

BREAKDOWN SHEET No.

LOCATION OR STUDIO

DAY OR NIGHT	D D D D D D D D D D D D D
SCRIPT PAGES	ToT 113 4/8
	AUG/DA 5 5/8 Pos

PROD No. **206747**
TITLE **STOLEN DREAMS**
P.M. **RON GROW**
PRODUCER **JACK GROSSBART**
DIRECTOR **FRANK DI VELITA**
ASST. DIRECTOR **DON HAVER**
CHARACTER / LAST CHANGE 12.9.85

COST / CHARACTER	No.	EXT HENRI - STILL	EXT HENRI? - STILL	EXT SAMANTHA H.	EXT JASON HOWELL STILL	EXT CAMPFIRE - 3rd PHOTO	EXT SAMS (KAREN) + S.GRAS	EXT SAMS KAREN/OTHER GIRLS		EXT WHARF/WATER/LUNCH	EXT RUSTIC LANDS & SEA	EXT DE/REZZA DOCK	EXT BEACH	MONDAY, JAN 6
SAMANTHA/KAREN	1		1	1		1	1	1		1	1	1	1	
JASON HOWELL	2				2					2				
FRANCESCA	3													
JIM ARMBRUSTER	4													
HENRI DELORCA	5	5	5				5	5						
D.A. HALE	6													
REINER	7													
DOBSON	8													
MICHAEL	9											11			
ALISON MORELAND	10			12										
TED ROBERTSON	11													
JOHNNY MATTHEWS	12													
MR WILKINS	13													
MRS WILKINS	14													
MONSIGNOR	15													
JUDGE	16													
FOREMAN OF JURY	17													
NEWSCASTER SC 295	18													
DOG - DUKE	D													
STUNTS PLAYBACK - OBER - PB	S													
GEMINI/SPLITSCEN	9/22										10 / A			
ATMOSPHERE	A													
MULTIPLE CAMERAS	MC									2C				
CARS	C													
BOATS	B									B	B	B		
EFFECTS	R/R													
CRANE	CR													
SCENES		12	69	81A	91A	170	65A	233	233	49 50 51	49 125	115 116	113 114	

(EXT RUSTIC lower: 127 to 135)

Notes:
- STILL SHOT HENRI
- STILL AT CHURCH
- STILLS FOR KAREN BEDRM
- STILLS FOR KAREN BEDRM
- A+H STILL PHOTO
- STILL FOR DENTIST OFF.
- STILL FOR DENTIST OFF.
- SISTERS
- KAREN RUNS TO BEACH CLOUD
- MEET MIKE w/BOAT
- WALK & THINK

STILL FRIDAY JANUARY 3, 1986

Scene Location	D markers	Scene #
EXT FALLING (MANSION)	D	1
EXT RODGERS PIER (CITY)	D	1
INT PRISON VISITING RM	D	
INT PRISON CORRIDOR	D	1
TUESDAY, JAN 7		
INT HOLDING RM	D	
INT HOLDING RM	D	
WED/JESSAY, JAN 8		
INT COURT RM (intimidation)	D	2
INT COURT ROOM	D	1 / 2 / 2 / 3 / 4
EXT EASTERN SEASIDE PK	D	2
INT ANTIQUE SHOP	D	1 / 4
INT ANTIQUES SHOP		1 / 2
INT ANT SHOP / BACKRM	D	1 / 2 / 3
WEEKEND / JAN 11-12	D	

Additional scene numbers / notes visible in grid:

Column	Notes
EXT FALLING (MANSION)	11
INT PRISON CORRIDOR	11
INT COURT RM (intimidation)	8 / 9 / 10? / 15 / 16 / 17 / G
INT COURT ROOM	5 / PB
INT ANTIQUE SHOP	24
INT ANTIQUES SHOP	18

Column	A/B/C/D letter marks
EXT RODGERS PIER	D
INT PRISON VISITING RM	PDM
INT PRISON CORRIDOR	5A
INT COURT RM	G / A
INT COURT ROOM	A
EXT EASTERN SEASIDE PK	A5
INT ANTIQUE SHOP	A / C
INT ANTIQUES SHOP	A / C
INT ANT SHOP / BACKRM	A

Column	B row
EXT FALLING	B
EXT RODGERS PIER	B
INT COURT RM	B
INT COURT ROOM	B
INT ANTIQUE SHOP	B

Column	Page count / numbers
EXT FALLING (MANSION)	20 / 15
EXT RODGERS PIER	291 / 292
INT PRISON VISITING RM	280
INT PRISON CORRIDOR	255 / 256
INT HOLDING RM	295 / PART I
INT COURT RM	277
INT COURT ROOM	243 / 244 to 269
EXT EASTERN SEASIDE PK	286 to 293
INT ANTIQUE SHOP	21 to 35
INT ANTIQUES SHOP	4 / 10 to 10
INT ANT SHOP / BACKRM	12 to 19

Bottom action descriptions:

EXT FALLING (MANSION)	WALK DOG TO BEACH / WATER
EXT RODGERS PIER	KAREN MEETS SAM ON BOAT
INT PRISON VISITING RM	JIM VISITS KAREN
INT PRISON CORRIDOR	JIM WALKS INT GUARD
INT HOLDING RM	JASON w/ KAREN
INT HOLDING RM	DIALOGUE FOR TV INT ANTIQUE SHOP
INT COURT RM	PER. SHOT OF SHOT / TRIAL STARTS
EXT EASTERN SEASIDE PK	KAREN JOGS TO SHOP
INT ANTIQUE SHOP	GET 15TH / JIM BRIEFS
INT ANTIQUES SHOP	TEST SAMANTHA SIGN
INT ANT SHOP / BACKRM	JES/WATCH TV / KISS

D   (DAY)

Sc. 105

     Bow of San Pablo in narrow river, going faster.

FILM INDEX

Title	Author or Adapter of Screenplay
The African Queen	James Agee, John Huston
Airport (1970, 1975, 1977)	Michael Scheff, David Spector, Don Ingalls, George Seaton
Alfie	Bill Naughton
All About Eve	Joseph L. Mankiewicz
All Quiet on the Western Front	George Abbott, Maxwell Anderson, Del Andrews, Lewis Milestone
All the President's Men	William Goldman
Anne of the Thousand Days	John Hale, Bridget Boland
Apocalypse Now	Francis Ford Coppola, John Milius
The Appaloosa	James Bridges, Roland Kibbee
Back to the Future	Bob Gale, Robert Zemeckis
Battle of Algiers	Franco Solinas
The Best Years of Our Lives	Robert Sherwood
The Bicycle Thief	Cesare Zavattini
Boomerang	Richard Murphy
Born Yesterday	Albert Mannheimer
Butch Cassidy and the Sundance Kid	William Goldman
The Caine Mutiny	Stanley Roberts
Casablanca	Julius J. and Philip G. Epstein, Howard Koch
The Chalk Garden	John Michael Hayes
The Champion	Carl Foreman
The Charge of the Light Brigade	Michael Jacoby, Rowland Leith
Citizen Kane	Orson Welles, Herman J. Maniewicz

Coal Miner's Daughter	Thomas Rickman
Coming Home	Robert C. Jones, Waldo Salt
A Connecticut Yankee in King Arthur's Court	Edmund Beloin
Craig's Wife	Mary McCally, Jr., George Kelly
Dead End	Lillian Hellman
Death of a Salesman	Stanley Roberts
The Detective (1954)	Thelma Schnee
Dial M for Murder	Frederick Knott
Dr. Doolittle	Leslie Bricusse
Dr. Strangelove or How I Learned to Stop Worrying and Love the Bomb	Stanley Kubrick, Peter George, Terry Southern
East of Eden	Paul Osborn
Elmer Gantry	Richard Brooks
The Entity	Frank P. DeFelitta
E. T., The Extra-Terrestrial	Melissa Mathison
The Exorcist	William Peter Blatty
A Fistful of Dollars	Sergio Leone, Duccio Tessari
The French Connection	Ernest Tidyman
Gandhi	John Briley
Gaslight	John Van Druten, Walter Reisch, John H. Balderson
The General	Al Boasberg, Charles Smith
Georgy Girl	Margaret Forster, Peter Nichols
The Glass Menagerie	Peter Berneis, Tennessee Williams
Gone to Earth (The Wild Heart)	Michael Powell, Emeric Pressburger
Gone with the Wind	Ben Hecht, Sidney Howard
Grand Hotel	William A. Drake
The Grapes of Wrath	Nunnally Johnson
The Great Escape	James Clavell, W. R. Burnett
Guess Who's Coming to Dinner	William Rose
The Guns of Navarone	Carl Foreman
Hamlet	William Shakespeare
Heaven's Gate	Michael Cimino
The Heiress	Augustus and Ruth Goetz
Henry V	Alan Dent, Laurence Olivier
Hiawatha	Arthur Strawn, Dan Ullman
High Noon	Carl Foreman
The Hospital	Paddy Chayefsky

Love Me or Leave Me	Daniel Fuchs, Isabel Lennart
The Magnificent Seven	William Roberts
The Maltese Falcon	John Huston
A Man and a Woman	Pierre Uytterhoven, Claude Lelouch
A Man for All Seasons	Robert Bolt
Marty	Paddy Chayefsky
The Misfits	Arthur Miller
Moby Dick	Ray Bradbury, John Huston
Morgan: A Suitable Case for Treatment	David Mercer
Mourning Becomes Electra	Dudley Nichols
Murder in the Cathedral	George Hoellering
My Dinner with Andre	Andre Gregory, Wallace Shawn
My Fair Lady	Alan Jay Lerner
The Naked City	Albert Maltz, Malvin Wald
Natural Enemies	Jeff Kanew
The Night of the Generals	Paul Dehn, Joseph Kessel
The Night of the Iguana	Anthony Veiller
Not as a Stranger	Edna and Edward Anhalt
Now, Voyager	Casey Robinson
Odd Man Out	F. L. Green, R. C. Sherriff
Oedipus Rex	W. B. Yeats (translation of Sophocles's play)
Of Human Bondage (1934)	Lester Cohen
Of Mice and Men	Eugene Solow
On Golden Pond	Ernest Thompson
Ordinary People	Alvin Sargent
Othello	Orson Welles
Our Town	Harry Chantlee, Frank Craven, Thornton Wilder
The Ox-Bow Incident	Lamar Trotti
Panic in the Streets	Edna and Edward Anhalt, Richard Murphy
Patton	Francis Ford Coppola, Edmund H. North
The Pawnbroker	Morton Fine, David Friedkin
Peter Pan	M. Banta, W. Hibler, B. Peet, E. Penner, J. Rinaldi, T. Sears, Ralph Wright
The Poseidon Adventure	Sterling Silliphant, Wendell Mayes

Track of the Cat	A. I. Bezzerides
Treasure of Sierra Madre	John Huston
The Trojan Women	Michael Cacoyannis
Two for the Road	Frederic Raphael
Two Minute Warning	Edward Hume
Under Milk Wood	Andrew Sinclair
The Verdict	Peter Milne
War and Peace (1956)	Bridget Boland, Mario Camerini, Ennio de Concini, Ivo Perilli, King Vidor, Robert Westerby
Who's Afraid of Virginia Woolf?	Ernest Lehman
The Wild Bunch	Walon Green, Sam Peckinpah
The Wind and the Lion	John Milius
Winterset	Anthony Veiller
Witness	William Kelley, Earl W. Wallace
The Wizard of Oz	Noel Langley, Florence Ryerson, Edgar Alan Woolf
Wuthering Heights	Ben Hecht, Charles MacArthur

INDEX

Index

Index

Index

Index